My *Memories* of the Youngest American Hero, PFC Dan Bullock

Dec 21, 1953 - June 7, 1969

NATHAN BULLOCK

PAGE PUBLISHING
Conneaut Lake, PA

First originally published by Page Publishing 2022

ISBN 979-8-88654-584-5 (pbk)
ISBN 979-8-88654-587-6 (digital)

Printed in the United States of America

Dan Bullock was born on December 21, 1953, in Goldsboro, North Carolina, to Alma Floyd Bullock and Brother Bullock, one of four siblings and the only boy (i.e., during this time period, if there was only one boy in the family, he could not enlist in the military) following Lois Mae Bullock, Porter Lee Bullock, Dan, and the youngest, Gloria Jean Bullock. He enlisted in the United States Marine Corps on September 18, 1968, in Brooklyn, New York. As a member of Platoon 3039 in Paris Island, he graduated boot camp on December 10, 1968, at the age of fourteen years old. Dan began his tour of duty in Vietnam on May 18, 1969, and he was killed in action on June 7, 1969, in An Hoi, Quang Nam Province, South Vietnam. At the time of his death, he was fifteen years old and a member of Fox Company, Second Battalion, Fifth Marine, First Marine Division. PFC Dan Bullock, fifteen years old, of the United States Marine Corps became the *youngest American serviceman killed in action in the Vietnam war.* According to pentagon officials, he may even be the *youngest killed in action since World War I.*

CONTENTS

ARTICLES WRITTEN ABOUT PFC DAN BULLOCK

PFC Dan Bullock

(Contributed by Steve Adams on Saturday, August 31, 2002)

Dan was the only son of Mr. and Mrs. Brother Bullock. Upon the death of Dan's mother, when he was twelve years old, his father moved the family to Williamsburg, Brooklyn. Mr. Bullock hoped for better opportunities for himself and his family. Dan on the other hand would have other plans. As a young boy, he dreamed of becoming a United States Marine, a pilot or a police officer. On September 18, 1968, Dan Bullock enlisted in the United States Marines, fulfilling one of his childhood dreams. Dan was just a young man with a dream. Upon his enlistment in the marines, Dan was sent to Parris Island, South Carolina, to begin basic training. On December 12, 1968, Dan graduated from Marine Corps Basic Training. For the next five months, Dan would receive more advanced training. On May 18, 1969, Private First Class

Dan Bullock was sent to Vietnam as a member of Fox Co 2nd Battalion, 5th Marines, 1st Marine Division. On June 7, 1969, at An Hoa Combat Base, An Hoi, Quang Nam Province, South Vietnam. "Just another Casualty of War, almost but not quite." At the time of Dan's death, his company commander, Captain R. N. Kingrey, United States Marine Corps, wrote to Dan's family the following:

"The recent death of your son, PFC Dan Bullock, United States Marine Corps, on June 7, 1969, An Hoa Combat Base, Quang Nam Province, South Vietnam, is a source of great sorrow to me and all the members of Company F. Dan was assigned as a Rifleman in the 2nd Plt of Company F. During the early morning hours of June 7, Co. F was in night defensive positions on the perimeter of the An Hoa Combat Base. An assault of the lines started at approximately 1:00 a.m. Dan immediately realized that the attack was stronger than usual and that the ammunition supply was becoming depleted. He rushed to get more ammo for his unit. He constantly exposed himself to the enemy fire in order to keep the company supplied with the ammunition needed to hold off the attack. As the attack pressed on, Dan again went to get more ammunition when he was mortally wounded by a burst of enemy small arms and died instantly at approximately 1:50 a.m."

This simple letter to Dan's parents reflects the heroism of PFC Dan Bullock. However, he has not been recognized for his heroism. In other circumstances, he would have, at the very least, been nominated for the "Medal of Honor" and/ or received the "Navy Cross" or the "Bronze Star," he did not. Circumstances dictated that he would not. Upon his death, Dan was returned home to Goldsboro, North Carolina, where he buried in a small cemetery in an unmarked grave where he would lie for more than thirty years. Thanks to the commitment of the PFC Dan Bullock Foundation, former United States Marines, like myself and Franklin McArthur, other veterans and veteran organizations, and especially Sally Jessy Raphael, the talk show host, Private First Class Dan Bullock would finally receive his headstone. On October 27, 2000, a caravan of veterans embarked on a journey from Brooklyn, New York, to Goldsboro, North Carolina, to place Dan's headstone at his grave. Along the way, we would receive escorts from several police departments, veteran organizations, including Rolling Thunder and Nam Knights. On October 28, 2000, after the United States Marine Corps denied our request for a military ceremony for Dan, the United States Air Force graciously performed the ceremony at the cemetery for Dan. Again, circumstance dictated the marines actions. By now, you may be wondering what the circumstances were that would cause the United States Marines to so dishonor one of their own. One who died heroically for his country. Private First Dan Bullock, United States Marine, deceased, is the youngest US Marine to die in battle since World War I. At the time of PFC Bullock's death, he was only fifteen (15) years old. Dan enlisted in the Marines at the age of fourteen. From the time Dan enlisted until his death, the marines did not know that he was underage, and Dan, despite his age, was in appearance quite the man. For several years, the PFC Dan Bullock Foundation has tried in vain to get the United States Marine Corps recognize Dan and to change their records regarding Dan being a fraudulent enlistment. While in fact this is true, in spirit, Dan was a marine through and through, and the bullets that killed Dan were not fraudulent, they in fact were very real. I have stared endlessly at Dan's photograph, asking myself what if Dan had not been killed in Vietnam what greatness could he have achieved both as a marine and as a person. This is a question we will never know. As the President of the United States and commander in chief, you have not only the power but the ability to right a wrong. Dan deserves his place in history despite his transgression. We have no desire to shame or embarrass the marines, for as former marines, the eagle, globe, and anchor flows through our blood. Had there been time under the circumstances, we believe that at the very least Dan would have received for the Navy Cross, Bronze Star, or, at most, he would have been nominated for the Medal of Honor. Mr. President, we respectfully request that you review the enclosed materials and, upon your review, should you believe that Dan is deserving of special consideration that his record as a fraudulent enlistment be either expunged or reflect his heroic actions in battle. We also request that Dan be recognized for his heroics in battle.

* * *

MY MEMORIES OF THE YOUNGEST AMERICAN HERO, PFC DAN BULLOCK

By Melanie D. Scott
INQUIRER SUBURBAN STAFF
(Posted on October 30, 2000)

On June 7, 1969, Marine PFC Dan Bullock was killed in a firefight at An Hoa Combat Base, in what was then South Vietnam. According to battle reports, Bullock and his unit were posted along the northern end of the base's airstrip about 2 a.m. when a regular North Vietnamese Army unit attacked them with rockets and mortars.

In the skirmish, Bullock and two other Marines were killed and 31 were wounded, including 19 who had to be evacuated. Chances are, Bullock would have been just one casualty among many.

His name is on Panel 23W, Row 96 of the Vietnam Memorial in Washington—except for one distinction: He was only 15 years old when he died. Perhaps even that would have been just a footnote in history, except for one former Marine who lives in Mount Laurel and who considered Bullock his best friend when their paths crossed in boot camp.

"He's a hero," said Franklin McArthur, who has launched a campaign to win special recognition for his Marine Corps brother. "He lied about his age to defend this country...

"He's the most patriotic young man. He took his secret to the grave to fight for an ideology, when you had grown men fleeing to Canada." McArthur helped organize a caravan that left Saturday from Brooklyn, N.Y., to travel to Goldsboro, N.C., where Bullock is buried.

McArthur has also established the PFC Dan Bullock Foundation, which is gathering money for a monument to the soldier to be erected in Brooklyn outside the Marine recruiting office where both men signed up.

Bullock is believed to be the youngest US soldier to die in Vietnam. He joined the Marines by forging his papers.

Saturday's trip ended with a dedication ceremony for a headstone for Bullock, who was buried without one in 1969. The headstone was donated by talk-show host Sally Jessy Raphael.

*Bullock lived in North Carolina until he was about 13, when his mother died and he and his younger sister, Gloria, moved to Brooklyn to live with their father and his wife.

"My brother didn't like New York," Gloria Bullock-Burroughs, 43, said in an interview. "He wanted to get an education, to make something of himself, and the Marines to get there."

"Changing his birth date from Dec. 21, 1953, to Dec. 21, 1949, to make it look as if he were 18, Bullock enlisted in the Marines and reported for duty on Sept. 18, 1968," McArthur said. Bullock was 14. He went to boot camp on Parris Island, S.C., and on May 8, 1969, arrived in Vietnam, attached to Fox Company, Second Battalion, Fifth Marines. A month later, he would be dead.

*The military's view of Bullock and other underage soldiers differs from McArthur's.

"We respect and appreciate their service, but they are part of the corps' fraudulent enlistees," said Maj. David Anderson of the Marine Corps' Division of Public Affairs. "They are part of the fold, and we recognize them, but [forging to enlist is] a violation of the Uniform Code of Military Justice." McArthur was 19 when he met

Bullock in boot camp, both members of Platoon 3039.

Although he was big and strong for his age, Bullock lagged behind during the daily run. "I got a group together, and we decided to carry him when he fell back," McArthur said. "I looked out for him." They last saw each other when they graduated from boot camp in December 1968.

McArthur learned of Bullock's death—and his age—while still in Vietnam from a front-page *New York Times* article that was circulated among Marines at the front. The June 13, 1969, article was headlined: "MARINE, 15, KILLED IN VIETNAM; ENLISTED AT 14, LYING ABOUT AGE."

"He shouldn't have died," Gloria Bullock told the Times reporter who visited the family's apartment in a "dilapidated" tenement in the Williamsburg section of Brooklyn. "He joined to help us out."

*Four years ago, McArthur visited the memorial in Washington and found Bullock's name.

"It still had his incorrect birth date listed," McArthur said.

He has petitioned the White House, Congress, and the Marine Corps not only to get Bullock's correct birth date listed but also to get him a Medal of Honor.

Although most Medal of Honor awards are given based on eyewitness recommendations, McArthur said he believed Bullock was entitled to the award because of his courage.

"He's a historical figure," he said. "My intention is to make everyone aware." McArthur also has placed notices on websites for veterans and an advertisement in a Marine publication, seeking anyone who knew Bullock in Vietnam. Steve Piscitelli, 50, answered.

He was surprised to find someone else who remembered Bullock. "No one had really known Dan," said Piscitelli, a sculptor in Orlando, Fla., who served with Bullock in Fox Company.

Piscitelli, the recipient of two Purple Hearts, said he also had looked after Bullock.

"He was an enigma. No one could figure him out," Piscitelli said.

The night Bullock was killed, he and Piscitelli had been sparring in a friendly fashion when Piscitelli broke his thumb. Bullock, who had been assigned to cleaning duty, went to the front-line post in Piscitelli's place.

Piscitelli, who became an artist as a way of dealing with post-traumatic stress, has worked with McArthur to design a statue that shows Bullock holding an M16 rifle in his right hand while positioning himself to toss, with his left hand, a grenade around the corner of a bullet-riddled wall. McArthur said Bullock's sacrifice was worth noting and wants to use Piscitelli's statue to do it. "He [Bullock] was remarkable… because he joined the corps and stood up for what he believed in and took his secret to the grave." (Melanie D. Scott's e-mail address is mescott@phillynews.com)

ACKNOWLEDGMENTS

I want to thank all the marines who served in Vietnam with PFC Dan Bullock, especially Steve Piticelli, who was Dan's closest friend while in Vietnam, and all those who sacrificed their lives and limbs, and all those who made it back and had to go through so much—the lack of understanding and respect shown to the Vietnam Veterans upon returning home, and to this very day, still is not given the respect, or medical attention, and the funds to live as a decent human being. I salute all the Vietnam veterans and acknowledge them all in every way that I can. I have posted quotes from the brave men that served alongside PFC Dan Bullock in Vietnam... *Semper fidelis* (Always faithful):

> I was with fox from May 16, 1969, to February 16, 1969. I was wounded a third time on February 10, 1970, by booby trap. I took out two corpsmen and a marine forward observer: although their wounds were not serious, mine were. I did a lot of walking point, ambush, patrol, etc. I carried the blooper for four months and also a M14 also for four months. I had a mohawk haircut and carried a buck knife. I'd like to hear from the men in my unit. I've been in touch with Kozy, Uncle, Blatchko, Mckinney, Lt. Hofmann, Peterson,

Sutton, and Elder. Anyone who remembers me or any of these men: please contact me.

Presently, I'm building a monument of Dan Bullock, who was 15 when he was killed on June 7, 1969. I also built a bronze Vietnam War Memorial in Bristol Township, PA. If anyone knows Roland Wolke, an artist from 2/5, please have him contact me. Semper fi. (Steve Piticelli)

* * *

I was there when Bullock got killed, the corn field, I remember David Micheals, Fuller, JJ, Booth, Rabbit, Wright, Balls, names and incidents that hadn't come up in quite some time. (Walker, Billy)

* * *

I was Fox 2/5 2nd platoon. I was in the rear with Dan Bullock when KIA. I have one or two picture of Dan. If someone want a copy, let know. August 1968–July 1969. (Williams, Wesley Y.)

* * *

I was with F 2/5 2nd Plt Sqd from March 1, 1969, to August 1969. I served with Steve Piscitelli, Dan Bullock, Egglinsdorfer, and Dan Farris.

Past this, I have forgotten a lot of names. I was at Charleston, SC, reunion but left early for health problems. I missed all I knew from my tiFox Co. by leaving. I was wounded the 3rd and 4th times in August '69. I was medivaced to Japan and returned to duty, finishing my 4 years at Marine Barracks Bermuda as a Sgt. I'd like to hear from all I served with. My memory is bad on names. It was a privilege and honor to serve with you all. See you in Reno, NV. (Dixon, Paul R.)

* * *

I went to 5th Marines summer 69. Was w/ 3/5 when Delta sector got hit and Dan Bullock was killed. Just a few hundred meters away but the Bn XO wouldn't let me take Re-Action squad to lines because of "5-day Acclimatization/Orientation" regs (my 5 days ended next morning!!!) So started my many "experiences" w/ SOP's & Red-Tape. Spent summer all over TAOR with I 3/5, then to F 2/5 in fall as 2d Plt Commander till end of '69 when finished tour w/G-5 Div HQ. Been in contact/met Piscitelli, Kozi (Kosibucki), Uncle, Blatchko, & Peterson. Hang out w/Steve Piscitelli since Statue Dedication in DC. We're coming to Re-union in Charleston, SC, July 2002. Semper fi...5th Marines: The Original Devil Dogs. (Hoffman, Robert)

Dec 21, 1953 - June 7, 1969

Hawaii Veterans of Foreign Wars (VFW) Post 911
http://www.vfwpost911hawaii.org/

Dedicated to the memory of PFC Dan Bullock, the youngest American serviceman killed in action in the Vietnam War.

> —Street Renaming Ceremony in Honor of
> PFC Dan Bullock (March 9, 2003)

On Saturday June 7, 2003, at the corners Nostrand Avenue and Flushing and Avenue, Brooklyn, New York, the PFC Dan Bullock Foundation and the city of New York will honor Dan Bullock by renaming Lee Avenue in honor of Dan Bullock, and we cordially invite any members of 2/5 Fox company or any other member of twenty-five to attend the street renaming ceremony in honor of PFC Dan Bullock.

> —USMC (deceased)

Date: Saturday, June 7, 2003
Time: 11:00 a.m.–1:00 pm.
Place: Nostrand Avenue and Flushing Avenue, Brooklyn, New York

COMMUNITY BOARD NO. 1

435 GRAHAM AVENUE - BROOKLYN, N.Y. 11211-2429
PHONE: (718) 389-0009
FAX: (718) 389-0098

HON. HOWARD GOLDEN
BROOKLYN BOROUGH PRESIDENT

VINCENT V. ABATE
CHAIRMAN

GERALD A. ESPOSITO
DISTRICT MANAGER

HON. KENNETH K. FISHER
COUNCILMAN, 33rd CD

HON. VICTOR L. ROBLES
COUNCILMAN, 34th CD

RABBI JOSEPH WEBER
FIRST VICE-CHAIRMAN

RONALD E. WEBSTER
SECOND VICE-CHAIRMAN

MINERVA MOSES
THIRD VICE-CHAIRPERSON

HAZEL T. HUNTER
FINANCIAL SECRETARY

BRUNILDA RIVERA
RECORDING SECRETARY

CHRISTOPHER H. OLECHOWSKI
MEMBER-AT-LARGE

(revised)
November 15, 2000

Councilman Ken Fisher
16 Court Street
Brooklyn, New York 11241

> **RE: Street renaming of Lee Avenue Between Wallabout Street
> and Flushing Avenue In honor of PFC Dan Bullock to
> PFC Dan Bullock Way**

Dear Councilman Fisher:

Please be advised that at the November 14, 2000 Board Meeting of Community Board No. 1, the members voted unanimously to support the request to rename a portion of Lee Avenue (the block at 279 Lee Avenue) between Wallabout Street and Flushing Avenue in honor of deceased PFC Dan Bullock, to PFC Dan Bullock Way.

The vote of the Board was as follows: 40 "YES"; 0 "NO"; 0 "ABSTENTIONS".

Attached please find a copy of CB #1's Transportation Committee Report that contain the biographical information on PFC Dan Bullock.

Working for a Better Greenpoint-Williamsburg.

Sincerely,

Vincent V. Abate
Chairman

VVA/mbw
Enclosures

TOTAL P.02

An Inherently Unfair System

Richard Nixon proposed ending the draft during the 1968 presidential campaign. Upon taking office, he immediately moved to eliminate the draft entirely. (AP Photo)

The worst single problem with the draft was that it was inherently unfair. In 1960, the US armed forces' total strength, counting both draftees and volunteers, was only 7.9 percent of the US male population, between the ages of eighteen and forty-five. No matter what, only a fraction of the eligible were drafted. Furthermore, there was great variation among local draft boards in how they applied the deferment and exemption rules. There was nothing equitable about the system for the minority of the manpower pool who did not escape the draft.

Washington in the mid-1960s made several attempts to establish a draft lottery to spread the risk of induction equally among those eligible for selection. Hershey was staunchly opposed, arguing that decisions by local boards were preferable to "blind chance" with a lottery. Johnson (then president) and Congress agreed, and the lottery initiatives failed. Also rejected was the idea of setting national standards for local draft boards to follow.

The draft was far from ideal as a source of military manpower. Because draftees served only for two years, it was not worthwhile putting them through long training programs. The technical specialties had to be filled with volunteers.

The Armed Forces Qualification Test (AFQT) ranked scores into five categories, with Category IV—scores in percentiles 10 through 30—being the lowest acceptable for military service. Cat IVs had difficulty absorbing instruction or performing complex tasks, but the draft brought many of them into service.

The number of Cat IVs increased between 1966 and 1971 as a result of Project 100,000—a program introduced by Secretary of Defense Robert S. McNamara. His aim was to open military service to one hundred thousand men a year, who were otherwise unqualified. By 1969, Cat IVs accounted for 23 percent of inductions.

The draft also brought in a larger number of high-school dropouts who, compared to graduates, were only half as likely to complete enlistments. In 1969, dropouts accounted for 27 percent of the enlisted force, ranging from a high of 42 percent in the marine corps and a low of 8 percent in the air force.

More than anything else, it was the Vietnam War that ended the draft. Inductions had fallen to 82,060 in 1962, but then soared to 382,010 in 1966. As draft calls increased, so did the probability that draftees would be sent to combat. Anti-draft sentiment grew, both among military age men and in the public at large. Performances by folksinger Joan Baez featured a banner that read, "Girls Say Yes to Boys Who Say No."

In time, the burning of draft cards as a form of protest became so widespread that Congress made it a felony. Some draft evaders went to Canada, but the more common way to avoid service was through deferments, exemptions, and disqualifications. Minorities and the poor were the least successful at beating the system this way. (Note: Not only did PFC Dan Bullock enlist at an early age, he took his secret to the grave with him.)

During the 1968 presidential campaign, Richard M. Nixon proposed ending the draft, and within days of taking office in January 1969, he took action to reduce the inequities. Secretary of Defense Melvin R. Laird told Nixon that the current requirement was to draft only about a quarter of the eligible men in the manpower pool, and that it would drop to 1 in 7 when the services reverted to pre-Vietnam strength levels.

Armed Forces as Percentage of Military Age Population

	Total Active Duty Forces	Male Population, 18 through 45
1950	1.46 million	4.8%
1953	3.56 million	11.6%
1955	2.94 million	9.6%
1960	2.48 million	7.9%
1965	2.66 million	8.0%
1969	3.49 million	9.8%

Source: Selective Service website

Laird proposed a lottery. Hershey was opposed, but Nixon agreed with Laird and obtained the concurrence of Congress. The draft lottery was implemented in 1969. At the same time, Nixon appointed the commission on an all-volunteer armed force with a charter to develop a plan to eliminate conscription. He chose as head of the panel former Secretary of Defense Thomas S. Gates.

"We have lived with the draft [for] so long that too many of us accept it as normal and necessary," Nixon said.

Hershey, who was opposed to the all-volunteer force (AVF), as well as the other reforms, was clearly part of the problem. Nixon did not hesitate to move against him. He promoted Hershey to four-star general, made him a presidential advisor, and replaced him as head of the Selective Service. Nixon paid no attention to the advice he then got from Hershey, who eventually was retired involuntarily in 1973 at age seventy-nine and after sixty-two years of military service.

The Gates Commission made its report in February 1970 and offered three main recommendations as the nation moved toward a volunteer force:

- A major increase in military pay.
- "Comprehensive improvements" in conditions of military service and recruiting.
- Establishment of a standby draft system.

A hidden tax in kind

It was clear to everyone that using the AVF would not be cheap, but the commission said that taxpayers at large had gotten a free ride with the draft force. There was a hidden "tax in kind" paid only by draftees and draft-induced volunteers, who were forced to serve for low pay. In 1970, pay for new recruits and draftees was about 60 percent of comparable civilian pay.

INTRODUCTION

Dan Bullock was born on December 21, 1953, in Goldsboro, North Carolina, in a section called "Little Washington," to Alma Floyd Bullock and Brother Bullock. Dan was one of four children: Lois, Porter, Dan, and Gloria. At the age of eleven, Dan's father moved his family from Goldsboro to Williamsburg, Brooklyn.

They lived at 279 Lee Avenue. Dan's dream of going into the military formed long before he went to Brooklyn, New York, as you will read in this book, Dan would fulfill his childhood dreams. Dan was rifleman assigned to the *Second Battalion, Fifth Marines, Foxtrot Company*. At the time of his death, Dan having realized that an attack by the North Vietnamese was much stronger than usual, and that the ammunition supply was becoming depleted. Dan rushed to get more ammunition, not once but twice, and it was upon his return the second time to rejoin his fellow marines that he was hit numerous times and was killed instantly.

PFC Dan Bullock, USMC, is the youngest United States serviceman killed in Vietnam and, according, quite possibly the youngest US serviceman killed in any war since World War I. At the time of his death, Dan Bullock was only fifteen (15) years old. Dan was killed on June 7, 1969, at An Hoa Combat Base, Quang Nam Province, Republic of Vietnam. Being the only boy in the family, even if Dan was eighteen, he would not have had to serve in the military at that time.

Today, PFC Dan Bullock, United States Marine, rests in the Elmwood Cemetery in Goldsboro, North Carolina, beside his mother (Alma Floyd Bullock) and grandmother, (Pinky Floyd), also his eldest sister (Lois Bullock Coleman).

May they all rest in peace.

CHAPTER 1

Memories/Little Washington

As I look back on the past, the best times of my life was when we lived on Griffin Street, a section called "Little Washington" on the west side of Goldsboro, North Carolina. I can vaguely remember the section called "The Big Road"; however, I do remember "The Horseshoe Bend." Everyone was like family; there were no strangers. In the 1960s, all the streets were dirt streets, and every so often, the road scraper (road grader) would come and level the dirt, which would push the red clay up to the top, and Dan and I would eat some; we were told that the red clay dirt would keep the worms out of our stomach (until this very day, I wonder if that was true, although I have never had worms in my stomach as far as I can remember).

We lived in a white one-story house that was big. The front porch was all the way across the front of the house and a spacious front yard with little grass. The back porch was in an L shape, and two back doors, and at the end of the back door that leads in the kitchen, we had a pantry with shelves and on those shelves were jars of preserves (i.e., peaches, plums, strawberries, etc.), fresh sausages, hams and other meats—with salt on the meat to preserve them, hanging up high on a raft to cure. We had the biggest garden in the backyard with rows of collards, corn, cabbage, tomatoes, watermelons, cantaloupes, cucumbers, beans, and peas.

In the back, on the left behind the kitchen, we had chicken coops that held hens and roosters in them; the coops were high up off the ground, in wire mesh screens. The chickens even had names; the one I remember the most was the meanest, and around the longest was a hen named "Big Red." She was in a coop by herself and would peck your hand when anyone sticks their hand inside the coop to get the eggs out. It was an art to snatching the eggs, speed and agility, which Dan mastered and taught me the same, which later became fun to do, and to this day, I love eggs no matter how they are cooked. It seems Momma was always in the kitchen cooking or cleaning; it's where she spent most of her time, but never alone. Tony and I was always with Momma when Daddy, Lois, and Porter were not at home and when Dan and Gloria were in school. We had a big cast-iron stove that we put wood in to cook and the heat the house. Daddy and Dan would cut the wood and pile it up by the stoves in the kitchen and in the front of the house where the other two stoves were. As I got older, Dan would cut the wood and let me stack the wood in a pile. We had a pump in the backyard. I used to watch Dan prime (i.e., pour water in the hole at the top of the pump, and pump the handle up and down really fast until the water would start to come out and into the bucket) the pump. He would fill the big water tub up full of water—water we used for cooking, cleaning, and for filling up the foot tub for us to take baths in.

Dan was the center of my world growing up. Back then, children did not get into grown folks' conversations. We had to go outside or in another room. So Dan and I spent a lot of time together, and he was teaching me something, or showing me something, which was always a learning experience. I know that Dan's biggest worry was about the headaches Momma seem to be having all the time, and he would talk to me about it all the time, especially when she would have us to go to the store to get her a Coca-Cola and Goody powder. Mr. Raymond had a store on the corner of Persimmons Street and Orchard Street. Mr. Jesse's store was on Canal Street and Orchard Street. Mr. Raymond's store was closer to our house, so Momma sent us there more often. However, when Dan and I went over to Aunt Leatha's, we always went to Mr. Jesse's store. Mr. Jesse would always be sitting on a tall stool behind the countertop with a big smile on his face, and his wife and daughter were always pleasant and seem to always be happy. And just like Mr. Raymond, Mr. Jesse would always give me extra cookies too. When Daddy would kill a hog, Momma, Lois, and Pete would sit out on the back porch and clean out the insides, and Daddy would put salt on the shoulders and hang them up at the end of the porch in the closet to let them cure. Back then, it seems Momma was always cooking or baking bread and cakes and humming the whole time.

Dan taught me how to swim in a place called the sand hole. The sand hole was across the truck lane (which is now Highway 117). I often look back and think of all the things that Dan taught me—like tying my shoes, boxing, how to shoot a BB gun, and make bow and arrows, popguns, and to make kites and fly them very high. I can remember Dan making trucks by driving nails into blocks of wood and tying a string of twine around the nails. He would nail the nail close to the edge of the wooden block, which was about four inches wide by eight inches long and one-inch thick. He would take the shorter block, which was also about four inches wide, four inches long, and one-inch thick. Dan would place the twine around the nails on each block, leaving several inches between the two so we can pull them on the makeshift roads that we created by dragging the garden tool called a "hoe" so that we could transport the soldiers from one destination to another one while we were playing war in our backyard.

More importantly, he taught me about family, and my namesake, "Bullock." Dan was really proud of our last name, and he loved our family. We had this big wooden box radio in the house, and it seemed to always be on, especially at night because we didn't have a TV then. We would listen to the news, sports, and music.

CHAPTER 2

World War II: In Our Backyard

Kaboom! Boom! Boom!

"The Japs are bombing us. Everybody, find a gun and start shooting at the planes. Hurry up, soldiers! Airplanes are everywhere, and they are trying to kill all of us Americans."

Boom!

"Come on! We got to fight back!"

Boom!

"Get the tanks loaded, aim it…now shoot it! Yeah! Yeah! It's on target. It hit right on that bull's-eye on that airplane. Look! That airplane is going down! Come on, reload. We got to shoot more of those airplanes down. They are everywhere!"

Kaboom! Aaaaarrrrraaagggggggg! Boom! Boom! Boom!

"Everybody, shoot at them planes! Get them tanks loaded. Hurry up, men! Keep shooting, men. We can't let them Japs kill us and take us as prisoners. We got to keep on fighting. Let's get our airplanes in the air too. Hurry up, men! Oh no! The Japs are crashing their airplanes into our ships! They must be running out of gas. We got to shoot them sown over the water before they can crash into our ships and kill somebody! Hurry, hurry, every soldier, everywhere, we got to fight back!"

Kaboom! Boom!
"Yeah, that's it y'all. Let's get them, Dan!

* * *

"Dan, come in here and bring Terry with you. I want you to go to Mr. Raymond's store for me. Tell him to give you a Goody powder and a coke, a quarters worth of cheese, a quarters worth of gingersnaps, and two pounds of white potatoes, and a loaf of bread. And Dan, you can get you and Terry some candy and some Kool-Aid to go with them cookies, for you Terry, Tony, and Gloria-Jean, okay?"

"Yes, Momma. Can I take Terry with me?" asked Dan.

"You can take him with you but hold his hand. You know how Lois is about him," she said, laughing while looking at her grandson.

"Yeah, I know, Momma. Ain't nothing gonna happen to him, ain't that right, Terry?"

"Yeah, that's right, Momma," answered Terry.

Dan said, "Come on, Terry, give me your hand. We're going to the store and get us some cookies and Kool-Aid."

"Dan, I like cookies and cheese too. Momma gonna give me some cheese too, ain't she, Dan?"

"Yeah, that's why she sent us to get them. She knows we got a war going on with the Japs in the backyard, and we got to eat a snack. Come on, let's hurry up, Terry, so we can get back before Lois and Pete get home."

"Where they gone at, Dan?" I asked.

"They went to put in tobacco, to make some money so Daddy won't get mad at them, and to make some money to buy stuff with."

"What kind of stuff, Dan?" I asked.

"Well, stuff like food, clothes, and shoes too. You got any more questions, Einstein?"

"Who is Einstein? My name is Terry."

Dan said, "Einstein is the smartest man in the world that they know of, and you are going to be smart too when you grow up."

"Yeah, I will be Terry Einstein."

"No, you won't. You will always be a Bullock, just like me, and I want you to always remember that too because we are Bullocks, okay?"

"What that mean, Dan?" I asked.

"Bullock is our last name. It is who we are, our family name, and it means we are proud, smart, and brave too."

"What brave mean, Dan?"

"Well, Terry; brave means strong, having a lot of courage, and doing the right thing under pressure, showing no fear at all like a warrior and a real soldier in combat. We are Bullocks, and we are brave too, okay?"

"Okay, Dan, I'm going in the store with you too, okay?"

"Yeah, come on in and say hello to Mr. Raymond. He might give us some extra cookies and cheese too, okay?" Dan opened the heavy screen door, leading Terry inside.

Mr. Raymond, always behind the counter, looked up and saw Dan and his little nephew come inside the store. As always, amazed at how fast Dan was growing and pleased with his mannerism, more like his momma Alma (such a lovely lady and pleasing to the eyes too), he smiled to himself, then quickly thought of Brother Bullock as Dan approached the counter, looking like his daddy, with that same intensity in his eyes that his daddy got. And the little one looking just like his daddy too, (yep, Desi Atkinson's boy for sure). With Desi being much older than his daughter Lois, it's a wonder Brother ain't shot Desi yet, but don't nobody mess with Desi any kind of way either. Brother sure was mad to find out Desi was messing around with Lois; she couldn't have been no more than fourteen or fifteen years old at the time, big for her age though.

Desi had to be in his twenties, around twenty-four or twenty-five years old, hard to tell because he's such a handsome fellow, and everybody can see that's his boy, looking like he spit him out. Pretty little curly-headed boy, always tagging along with Dan, which seems to please Dan, having a little brother or nephew.

"Hey, Mr. Raymond," Dan said, startling him as the little one chimed in, "Hey, Mr. Raymond."

"How are you boys doing today, Dan?"

"Sir, we're doing fine. My momma sent us to get a pack of Goody powder, a coke, and a quarter's worth of cheese, a quarter's worth of gingersnaps, a loaf of bread, two pounds of potatoes, some grape Kool-Aid, and some candy for us too. My momma said for you to put it all on the books for her, Mr. Raymond."

"Okay, is that all, Dan?"

"Yes, sir, that's all she told me, Mr. Raymond," replied Dan.

"Okay, it's going to take me a minute. Dan, how about you getting some of those Irish potatoes out of that basket for me, son, and put about eight or ten in this, here scale, and let's see if that's about two pounds. You know how to do it, son, don't you?"

"Yes, sir, Mr. Raymond."

"Son, can you count to 50?"

"Who? Me?" I asked.

"Yes, can you count?"

"His name is Terry Bullock, and he can count, Mr. Raymond. I taught him, did I not, Terry?"

"Sure did. What do you want me to count for you, Mr. Raymond?"

"Well, how about stepping up on that bucket right here and help me count out fifty of these gingersnap cookies, okay?"

"Yes, sir, Mr. Raymond… One, two, three, four…"

Once Mr. Raymond gathered everything up, he said, "Terry, since you can count really good, I am going to give you five extra cookies for being such a big help to me."

"Thank you, Mr. Raymond."

Dan said, "Terry, you take this bag, and I will take the heaviest bag. Come on, let's go."

"Dan, how old is Terry now?" Mr. Raymond asked.

Dan said, "He is almost five now and growing up fast too."

"He looked just like Desi, don't he?"

Dan ignored Mr. Raymond. "Come on, Terry, let's go back home so Momma won't worry about us."

"Who is Dee, Dan?"

"Don't you worry about who he is. We'll get back home, we can eat some cookies and cheese and drink some Kool-Aid, then we can play war some more in the backyard, okay?"

"Yeah, we can shoot all of them planes down, Dan."

"We got to make some trucks and army jeeps too, okay?"

"How we gonna make them, Dan?" I asked.

"We would use some word and stream. I will show you when we get home, don't worry. Come on Einstein," Dan said, laughing.

As we turned off School Street, onto Griffin Street, the street we lived on, Dan said, "Hey, come on, hurry up. See that truck? Lois and Pete are home from working in tobacco. Get over here on this side of the road. Here comes that old truck."

As the truck passed, the horn blew, and female voices were yelling, "Hey, Dan! Hey, Terry! And Dan, when you gonna come out and work with us? You're show is big enough!" from inside the truck, then laughter erupted.

As we went inside, we could hear Momma in her sweet voice, "Lois, you, and Pete, go on and wash up, animated by the time you both finished, I'll be through cooking. Won't we, Gloria?"

"Yes, ma'am," said Gloria.

"And it may be Dan and Terry will be back too."

Dan said, "Momma, we are already back, and we weren't gone long and got everything you told us to get to."

"Thanks so much, Dan. Come, cut you and Terry some of that cheese and get some of those gingersnap cookies. Gloria, come here and get you and Tony some of these cookies. Where is my Goody powder and coke? My head is hurting, some kind of bad child," said Momma.

"Momma, you need to go to a doctor about those headaches. You are not supposed to have headaches all the time," declared Lois as she entered the room.

"Girl, I'll be all right in a few minutes. Help Gloria peel some of those potatoes. She's been busy all day long with Tony and helping me out. She needs to be outside, playing like the other little girls," said Momma.

"Gloria, you can go on outside. I'll finish those potatoes. Pete is giving Tony a bath, so don't worry. Go have some fun, sweetie," Lois said, rolling her big brown eyes at Momma, sparking a smile from her.

"Terry, did you miss me today, baby?" asked Lois.

"I ain't no baby. I am a big boy. Me and Dan gonna be soldiers. Brave soldiers too! Ain't we, Dan?"

"Yes," Dan said while laughing. "Come on, Terry, let's go back outside. We got a war to win, soldier."

Once outside, Dan explained how to make bombs. "We got to use the garden hoe to chop the dirt so we can make some more bombs, but first, we got to get all the matches up. Terry, you get the big matches up, and I'll get the little ones. These are our soldiers. And when we get them all up, we'll place them so the bombs from the Jap's airplanes won't kill so many of our soldiers. Then we got to make some trucks and jeeps. Okay, now that we got all the soldiers up, we got to place them like this"—Dan was putting the small matches into the holes that he created with the axe and the garden hoe—"so put the big matches next to some of the little ones, okay?"

"Dan, I got all mines. Now what we going do?" I asked.

"The big ones will be the officers, and the little ones will be the soldiers because we don't have a lot of big ones left. We will get some more when we go back to Mr. Raymond's store, okay?"

"Okay."

"Come on, Terry, let's get some wood to make the trucks and jeeps. Here is the kind we need, the flat ones, short and long, like these," Dan said while holding up a long piece of wood and a short piece to give his young nephew an idea of what he meant. "I am going to go get the hammer, nails, and some tacks. And we are gonna need some twine too. I'll be right back. You just keep on looking for some flat pieces of wood and put them right over here in a little pile, okay?"

"Okay," I said.

Dan was back in a jiffy. "Hey! I got everything we need, Terry. Come here so I can show you how we are going to make jeeps and the trucks. You see, we got to put a tack up front here and in the middle of this long piece of wood, and then in the middle of the short piece of wood here, but only in the back because the short one will be in the front of the truck. Now let me tie this twine together in a knot. He can't be too long. See? Now you put it like this, and both pieces were moved at the same time," Dan explained. "Now these little pieces, we can just make them into jeeps. These holes like this, they are called foxholes. This is where soldiers can get in and hide so the Japs can't see them or kill them. It's safer. Terry, watch this." Dan picked up a clump of dirt, got back up, started a sound like a plane—*Aaaauungggg*—then threw a clump of dirt. *Kaboom*! "Now, let's check the soldiers. See, but they are not broken, so they are still alive. I told you, didn't I?" said Dan.

Dan said, "Terry, come here. You stand over there, and you throw dirt over here and try to kill my soldiers, and I'll dirt over there and try to kill your Japs, okay?"

I said, "Why do I got to have the Japs? I want the American soldiers. I ain't no Jap, Dan."

Laughing, Dan said, "Come on, Einstein, we are just playing, and I can throw harder than you, so I can kill those Japs better, okay?" Dan said. "Are you ready!" shouted Dan.

"Yeah, I'm ready!" shouted Terry.

"One, two, three, go!"

Kaboom! Kaboom! Boom!

"Hey! Hey! What are y'all doing? Stop that right now. Dan, both of you boys, stop it!" said Daddy.

Dan responded by saying, "Daddy, we're just playing war. Momma said we can play right here, just not to get into garden."

"Okay, but going over there and get them eggs out them coops, then wash them down. Don't let them chickens peck you either, especially old red. How are you doing, boy?"

"My name is Terry Bullock!" I said.

"I know your name. You sure are a Bullock. What have you been doing today?" Daddy asked.

"Me and Dan been playing war, and we went to Mr. Raymond's store too!"

In the meantime, Dan went inside and got the egg basket, and let Momma know that Daddy was home and wanted him to get the eggs out of the chicken coop and wash them. In case she needed him to do anything for her, he asked her before he left, "Momma, do you have enough firewood for the stove?"

"Baby, I got enough, so don't you worry about that tonight. Thank you anyway. Dan, tell your Daddy to come in here for a minute," said Momma.

"Yes, ma'am," said Dan.

"Daddy, Momma wants you to come here for a minute. Terry, come on over here with me so you can watch me get these eggs, okay?"

I said, "I can get them real fast, Dan. Ask Momma, she lets me get them," I said.

Dan said, "Yeah, well you just watch me this time, so we can hurry up and finish, then we can go eat and play some more. Come on. See that chicken, the big red one? You got to watch her. She is mean. She doesn't want nobody to mess with her eggs, so I got to get them really fast, and it is five eggs in there too, so move back and watch me." Dan opened the cage door, and in a flash, he grabbed two eggs and close the cage door before the big red hen could hardly react to the invasion of her domain. After placing the two eggs in the egg basket, Dan opened the cage door again and, just as quickly as the first time, snatched too more eggs and then the last egg in a split second. Every time Dan stuck his hand into the cage, Big Red tried to peck his hand, but Dan was too fast.

"Dan, that was really fast," I said in amazement.

As we moved to the next chicken coop, Dan said, "Terry, these chickens in here are nice, and it is easy to get their eggs. Watch this." Opening the door, Dan reached inside, taking two eggs at a time until he had all seven of them, before moving onto the next chicken coop, and until he got the eggs out of all seven chicken coops, getting a total of twenty-three eggs.

"Come on, Terry, let's go over to the water pump and rinse these eggs. Also, we can take them inside and give them to Momma." Dan got the bucket, placed it under the pump, and said, "Here, you get on this bucket, take this jug of water, and pour it right in this hole while I pump so we can get the water flowing. This is called priming the pump, so don't forget that, okay?" said Dan.

"Okay, I already know because I do it with Momma. She told me how to do it before," stated Terry.

As Dan pumped and Terry poured the water, after only three or four pumps, the water came gushing out, filling up the bucket. After rinsing the eggs off and filling the bucket up again, Dan carried the bucket over to the chicken coop, and instead of dashing the waterside, he poured the water a little at a time so he wouldn't disturb the chickens too much, watching the waste wash away, moving from one chicken coop to the other, until he was finished. Terry, sitting over on the start, watching them like a hawk, asked, "Dan, you finished?"

"Yeah, come on, let's go wash our hands and face so we can go inside and eat."

While washing their hands, Lois yelled, "Dan, you and Terry better come on in here so y'all can eat!"

"She yelled all the time, don't she, Dan?" I asked.

"Well, she just wanted to make sure we hear her, that's all," said Dan.

As we entered the kitchen, we could smell the fried chicken and see, Lois, Pete, and Gloria fixing their plates and ours too. Momma and Daddy was sitting out front on the porch. Pete had Tony in her lap, feeding him small pieces of chicken. Lois helped Terry to the table and gave him a plate, kissing his face, knowing he didn't like to be treated like a baby. We all laughed at his reaction. Lois asked Dan to bless our food because he is the man of the house when Daddy is not present, something momma started a few years ago when Dan was only seven years old and something that he took very seriously ever since that first invitation. Dan said, "Will everybody please bow their heads? Dear Lord, we ask that you bless our family and the food we are about to receive, and will you stop Momma's stomach from hurting all the time. Please, Lord, amen."

"Boy, there ain't nothing wrong with Momma's stomach," said Pete.

Dan said, "Her stomach does hurt all the time. She just doesn't want nobody to know."

"Dan, what do you mean she doesn't want nobody to know? It might just be that time of the month, and women don't like to talk about that, especially around men, much less than her own son."

Dan looked at Pete and shrugged, knowing that she did not understand, and do better than to not get in a fuss with her, so he turned his attention to the plate of food before him and began to eat his dinner solemnly.

In order to break the silence, Lois asked, "Gloria, what have you been doing all day?"

Gloria said, "I've been helping Momma around the house, and when we start back school, I am going to go to the school Dan goes to, and when I get big, I am going to go to college. I can already count to 100 and start all over and get a 200 and keep on going to a thousand and even more because Dan taught me, and now I'm teaching Terry."

Pete said, "Oooh girl, you are smart, and you just love to talk too, don't you?"

Lois, annoyed, said, "Leave her alone, Pete. She doesn't love to talk no more than you do or anybody else."

Dan, looking and listening, finally decided to speak up, "Gloria Jean is smart, and she can go to college when she gets old enough and make something of herself, and I will help her too. You just wait and see!"

Everyone seemed to get quiet and just ate as if everyone was lost in their own thoughts—thoughts about their own futures. Lois, noticing the glacial silence, decided to speak up to break the somber mood, "Dan, what about you? You gonna work in the lumber yard with Daddy when you get grown?"

"No, I ain't! I'm going to go in the army and fight for my country and be a brave soldier and hero. You just wait and see."

Pete said, "Boy, you always talking about a war and fighting in the White man's army. Them white people don't care about you, Dan, and no other Negro either. Besides, ain't no White man gon' call no Negro boy no damn hero. You need to think about getting a job with Daddy when you get old enough to work and stop thinking about going off to a damn White man's war somewhere in some other country, and you gonna see that it's a Black and White war going on right here in America, and it's been going on for hundreds of years, and you talk about a damn hero. Boy, you just as crazy as can be."

Lois, looking around, could see that it was time to intervene, although Dan didn't seem shaken. Terry and Gloria, while fidgeting and has stopped eating, Lois said, "Pete, leave him alone and quit cussing so much. He's young. Let him dream, and anyway, by the time he's eighteen years old, he might change his mind. And if they don't, the army might be different, and I heard Daddy and Big Dave talking about some Black soldiers who were heroes, called the Buffalo soldiers, as some of the Black airplane pilots, flying planes in the war, and they were heroes, so he might be a hero one day if he sets his mind to it, so let him be."

Pete said, "Girl, you always taking up for him!"

"That's cause you always messing with him," said Lois.

Dan got up and went outside to get away from the bickering and walked around to the front of the house, where he found Momma and Daddy sitting on the front porch as they usually did in the evenings. Sitting down on the steps, Dan asked, "Daddy, was they Black soldiers in the army that was called Buffalo soldiers?"

"They sure was, son, and they were the bravest of the brave too. I believe they were formed about a hundred years ago and even fought in World War I and World War II, son."

Dan asked, "What about Black soldiers flying airplanes, is that true, Daddy?"

Daddy looked at Dan and knew he was really serious seeking an explanation, or information, as he usually did. Daddy said, "Sure enough, son. Overseas, they used to fly planes to escort them big ole cargo planes, which flew supplies from one place to another, even in war zones. Those Black pilots would fly right beside them big ole cargo planes and shoot down the enemy planes, who were trying to shoot down the cargo planes so they couldn't get the supplies to the troops that needed them really bad. And you know what, son, them Black pilots never ever lost one of them big ole cargo planes. They are called the Tuskegee Airman, out of Alabama. And boy, them some real heroes."

Dan said, "Daddy, Pete don't know what she is talking about. Ain't no White man gon' call no Black soldier a hero, do she?"

"Well, son, they sure don't want to, that's for sure. Those White folks sure hate Black folks, and they're mean too, most of them anyway. Some of them still act like its slavery time. You got to be careful around them, I tell ya. But change gon' come, even if I ain't here to see it, but you'll be here, Dan. You want to go in the army when you grow up, don't you, Dan?"

Dan answered, "Yes, sir!" Looking all serious, standing straight and tall, chest sticking out as if he were at attention, like a soldier.

"Well, you always talking about it. Be about eight more years since you be ten in December on your birthday. You got to be eighteen years old before you can join the army. You will be bigger and stronger by then and smarter too."

Not liking the answer, Dan, asked, "Why?"

Looking at his son and deliberately taking his time as though giving it a serious thought, finally he said, "Because you got to be grown boy, and you ain't grown till you turn eighteen years old."

Dan, feeling dejected, stood up and walked toward the back of the house, thinking that eight years was a long, long way off from now. So lost in thought, he didn't hear Momma ask if he got enough to eat.

As Dan reached the side of the house, he saw Terry coming out of the kitchen door; and before he could speak, Terry began to fire off rounds of verbal bullets in the form of question marks. "Dan, where you been? Want to play some more war? You not tired, are you?"

Dan said, "Yeah, come on. I was just coming to get you so we can play some more war, Terry. We got to put the soldiers in the trucks and transport them to the duty stations, okay?"

I asked, "What does transport mean, Dan?"

Dan said, "It means to carry the soldiers from one place to another, like those black Tuskegee airplane pilots had to transport cargo and supplies to one place to another. That's how they get there. They can walk or go by airplane or trucks, so we gonna transport our soldiers by trucks. That's why we made the army trucks. Terry, you take these matches, line the little ones up on the truck, and I will put someone this truck, and then we'll put the big ones on the trucks too. Remember, the big ones are the officers, and the little ones are the soldiers, like the Buffalo soldiers. They are the bravest of the brave, and they are heroes too. Now, just lay them down like this. See how I'm doing?"

I said, "Yeah, I see, like this?" Terry began to place the wooden matches on the wooden made trucks, just as he saw Dan doing.

"That's right. You did just like I'm doing. Now let's drive them over there, and then stick them in the foxhole so they can hide when the bombs get to dropping out of their airplanes, okay? I will take mine over this side here, okay? Let's go, soldier! All right, soldiers, get in the trucks. We're going to the war zone. Everybody, make sure you've got enough bullets and hand grenades. Check your water and food soldiers. We might be gone a long time, and some of us might not make it back. Y'all knew that when you signed up for the army. But don't worry, we are well trained and ready to go to war, and we will win soldier's because we are fighting for our country. What's our country? America!" Dan was yelling, and when he yelled the second time, "What's our country!"

Terry yelled with him, "America! America! America!"

We sat in the dirt next to Momma's garden and pushed the wood trucks through the dirt, making sounds like two-ton trucks and sounds like jeeps make, pushing one truck forward a few feet, then sliding back to bring another truck up to the other one. This Dan called a convoy. Dan yelled, "Everybody, out! Get out, soldiers. Hit the foxholes! Hurry! hurry! Officer Terry, get those soldiers in the foxholes before the planes get here. I'll set up the tanks so we can shoot them down. Okay? Do you hear those planes coming? Get all the soldiers ready! The Japs are back; here they come, get ready! Shoot them down!"

Aaaaannnngggggg! Kaboom! Boom! Boom!

"Soldiers, shoot them planes down, turn them tanks around, hurry up before they come back. Hurry! Hurry, soldiers!

"Dan! Terry! Now come on in. It's getting dark, and y'all need to get in here and get a bath!" Lois yelled.

"Girl. We're coming. You ain't got to yell so loud like that," said Dan.

"Boy, you better come on before Daddy comes back here and get you. Momma told me to come back here and get you and Terry, and look at you, Terry, with you dirty self. Both of y'all are dirty. Terry, you come on now so I can give you a bath, back there laying on the ground messing up your clothes like that. And Dan, Momma said to get some water and bring it in here, so fill that bucket up, okay? Thanks, sugar, you know I love you," Lois said as she and Terry went inside.

Dan took the bucket and placed it under the pump and began to pump water into the bucket.

Overhead, Dan heard an airplane and knew it was going to Seymour Johnson Air Force Base, only a mile or so away, because he had been out there on a field trip with the E. A. House Boys Club, with Dave, and even got to sit in a real B-52 bomber. And the thought of Black people flying airplanes let him know that someday he would at least fly in one, when he went into the army someday. As the airplane went overhead, he marveled at the loud powerful sound the airplane made and wondered if it was the same B-52 bomber he sat in just a few weeks ago. Dan listened until he couldn't hear the airplane anymore, then began to pump more water into the bucket, smiling to himself, daring to dream, unlike most ten-year-old boys, and so full of pride…

CHAPTER 3

Boxing

Dan loved boxing, and when Cassius Clay made his debut in the Olympics of 1960, he knocked out most all of his opponents. Dan would listen to the reports on the radio and read all that he could in the newspapers. He always talked about how bad he wanted to see Cassius Clay box on television (we did not have a television; not many Blacks had televisions in the 1960s where we lived) and in person someday. He would tell me how he thought Cassius Clay would beat all the top heavyweight contenders, even Floyd Patterson and Sonny Liston. (And sure enough, Cassius Clay took the belt from Sonny Liston on February 25, 1964, becoming the youngest to ever win the Heavyweight Championship at the age of twenty-two years old. The referee stopped the fight after the sixth round because of a cut over Sonny's left eye that would not stop bleeding. Sonny's corner threw in the towel at the start of the seventh round, proclaiming, "I am the greatest. I am the king.")

Daddy loved boxing and thought Dan could be a professional boxer or whatever he wanted to be in this world. I used to listen to Daddy talk to Dan about boxing and an array of other topics. Having three girls, Daddy always seemed to be proud of Dan and enjoyed having a son to share his history, thoughts, and desires with so that he could pass them on to the next generation. I used to hear them talking about boxing. Daddy use to tell Dan about Joe Louis (the Brown Bomber) and Sugar Ray Robinson. Daddy didn't like Rocky Marciano, but Dan said he did respect that Italian boy because he is incredibly good, but that he just wasn't Black. Dan would always tell me what he and Daddy talked about because I was not included in their conversations most of the times, or he would run me in the house or another room. Dan would talk to ole Big Dave about boxing too.

Big Dave was the biggest man I have ever seen; he was huge. He was always smiling, and everyone seemed to like him and enjoy talking with him. Big Dave always wore blue jeans coveralls, with one side of the top flap unhooked so it hung down; we always joked that it was too tight for him. He wore big black shinny boots every day, even when it was raining. Big Dave owned a shoeshine stand on the Block. He would talk to Dan about boxing and teach Dan how to box on occasions. He would hold his giant arms out, with his palms out, and tell Dan to hit them.

"Left jab, left jab, left jab, plant, now over hand right. Yeah, that's it, Dan. Left hook to the body, now double up, now left hook to the head, step back, throw that overhand right. That's it, knock out. You knocked him out, now we gonna work some combinations, and when he comes in, how to rock his world when he is on his way out, so get in your south paw stance this time. There you go. You ready? We gonna do just the opposite. You got to be versatile in order to be a great boxer," said Big Dave.

"I am going to go in the army when I get old enough and learn hand-to-hand combat. I like boxing, but I'd rather fly a plane like the Tuskegee Airman did so I can be a hero too. I want to box better now so I can protect the family and myself as best as I can. I don't want my sisters trying to stick up for me every time they think something happened to me, like when I got shot with that bottle cap on the arrow. That was nothing, and Pete wanted to go around there and jump on them. They think I can't take up for myself, and I look out for Terry when he goes somewhere with me. I know how to fight. I just don't like to fight. It seems that all the fights I see are just stupid and for nothing. Nobody seems to end up winning unless it's for respect. Sometimes, people fight just to be fighting. I guess they're just mean. Pete acts like she loves to fight, especially on Lois. And Lois don't like to fight, but she will, and she will take up for Pete too. She can beat Pete up, but she doesn't want to hurt her. She loves everything and everybody. Pete took after Daddy, and Lois took after Momma. I guess I take after both of them put together," Dan said.

Big Dave listened to Dan and could see how serious he was. He knew that sparing with him would relieve some of his stress, so he stood up off the steps and said, "Come on, Dan, let's finish. We've been talking long enough. Time to get back to work."

Dan jumped up and walked toward Big Dave.

"This time I want you to start out throwing jabs with your right hand," said Big Dave.

I just sat on the steps of the big barrel and watched as Dan did what Big Dave told him to do, and it seemed that Dan was doing it before Big Dave could finish saying what he wanted Dan to do.

Dan never said anything, just kept on doing what Big Dave instructed to him to do.

"All right now, let's work on the body and the head at the same time. Come on. Left jab, left jab, hard right hook to the body, now hard right hook to the head. All right now, let's do it faster. Left jab, left jab, hard right hook to the body, now hard right hook to the head. That's what I'm talking about, Dan. Boy, you a natural. You gonna be good at boxing."

"Big Dave, have you ever seen Floyd Patterson box before?" Dan asked.

"No, but I listen to him fight Sonny Liston on the radio last year, when Sonny knocked him out in the first round. A lot of people felt like Floyd took a dive because he was afraid the mafia would kill him and his whole family, or that he was paid more money to lose by taking a dive, but that was, and still is, a lot of talk. Sonny outweighed him about twenty-five pounds, and he hit harder too. That fight never really got started before it was over with. Floyd was trying to feel Sonny out and got caught fooling around, I suspect," Dave said.

"Well, what do think about Cassius Clay?"

"I believe he can beat both of them, and anybody else he fights. I heard him on the radio, and he said ain't nobody alive can beat him."

"I believe him too, Big Dave," stated Dan.

Big Dave was looking at Dan with a smile on his face, knowing Dan was waiting for a response. He said, "Well, son, I didn't think nobody could whup the Brown Bomber either. But that Italian fellow, Rocky Marciano, knocked him down twice before knocking him out in the eighth round. Clay concerns me a little because he talks too much. But a lot of people like him, and so far, he is backing up his words. He takes care of business once he is in the ring though. He beat all of them White boys overseas and won that gold medal. He is a hero now, and folks will never forget that he will go down in history too. He beat that British champion. I believe his name is Cooper. After he beat some other boxers, and I'll just say he won against Sonny Liston making him the Champ, but I believe Sonny Liston will beat him the next time they fight. I will always wonder what would've happened if the referee wouldn't stopped that fight. He'll probably beat Sonny Liston again, but I won't believe it until I hear or see it. That's just my belief, son, but we'll see maybe next year sometime. He's young and will probably beat anybody else too, especially if he learns to control that mouth. He is big, strong, fast on his feet, and cocky too." Big Dave started laughing in that deep baritone of his. "They say Malcolm X was at his fight against Sonny Liston. He will become a Muslim soon, if he ain't one already. I know one thang, he won't be taking no dives for no mafia. Not if he is hanging with Malcolm X, that's for sure."

Dan said, "Big Dave, I can't tell if you like Cassius Clay or not. You speak good about him one minute and bad the next. But I think you like him. You just got to get use to him, and you just wait, he will beat Sonny Liston again too. And I like Malcolm X."

"Dan, it's just that I learned a long time ago to take a look at all sides, and sometimes, you just have to wait to see how things gon' turn out. That way you don't get cha feeling hurt way too bad, that's all. And whatcha know about Malcolm X?" asked Big Dave.

"Well, I listen to him on the radio with Daddy when he gives a speech, and my teacher tell us about him too. I remember when he said, 'We declare our right on this earth…to be a human being, to be respected as a human being, to be given the rights of a human being in this society, on this earth, in this day, which we intended to bring into existence by any means necessary.' And he said, 'Our objective is complete freedom, justice, and equality by any means necessary.' But my teacher told us he said, 'Without education, you're not going anywhere in this world.' Also, 'Education is our passport to the future, for tomorrow belongs to the people who prepares for it today,'" said Dan.

Big Dave started laughing, then he said, "Dan, now that's real smart of you. But I don't want you to be some kind of militant, like a lot of these young boys running around here, so you just concentrate on what Malcolm X said about education and apply that to your life so you will be prepared for your future. Me, myself, I choose to follow Rev. Martin Luther King Jr., which is the nonviolent way because ain't nothing never gon' be settled by being violent. Malcolm X talking about by any means necessary, talk like that can stir up some violence if you ask me. Well, I am a little tired now, so we gonna have to pick up on this some other time. I would offer you a drink, Dan, but you are still too young, and I don't want no beef with your Daddy or nobody else. And I want you to watch my backyard when I ain't here, and if you see somebody back here, don't say nothing to them. Just let me know who it was, and I will have a talk with them. I can tell somebody going in my barrels and getting some of my alcohol out of it. They ought to have a swollen belly because it won't even ready yet." Big Dave let out a big booming laugh, sounding like big ole Mr. Jesse. "Dan, you and ole curly head take this Kennedy fifty-cent piece and go the store and buy y'all something," said Big Dave, handing Dan a shiny big fifty-cent piece.

"I sure will, Big Dave, and thanks for teaching me how to be a better boxer and for the money too," said Dan.

CHAPTER 4

―――――

Hand-to-Hand Combat

The next morning, I heard momma called Dan, so I went to her bedroom, and Dan was already there. She was saying, "You and Terry, go on, hurry back because I got a headache."

Dan said, "Yes, ma'am."

When Dan got outside, Dan said, "Momma needs to go see a doctor because she always seems to be in pain, or in a headache, it ain't right! Come on, Terry, let's walk fast so we can hurry back home. We got to get Momma a BC powder and a coke. Why you so quiet? No questions, Einstein?"

"Yeah, I got a question. Momma ain't sick, is she, Dan?" I asked.

Dan looked down at Terry and saw the stern look in his eyes as Terry looked up at him, waiting for an answer. Dan said, "I don't know. She doesn't laugh and smile the way she used to laugh and smile. It's like her head is hurting all the time now, but she will be fine. She always prays to God, and you know he listens to her. She's gonna be fine, so don't you worry."

As we walked down Orchard Street, we passed by this big white house, and these pretty girls were on the porch and looking at us, and the big girl said, "Hey, Dan and Terry."

Dan said, "Hey, Linda!"

Those other girls started laughing and kept one looking at us.

I said, "Those girls always looking at us when we walked by their house. They just look and don't say nothing, and then they laugh and giggle. Ole silly girls, but Linda always speaks. She likes you, don't she, Dan?"

Laughing, Dan said, "Those little girls like you that's why they be looking at you and saying how cute you look with all that curly hair. They like you, Terry. Look at you looking back at them. You like them too."

"Hey, come on! There's Pa Wright!"

Pa Wright and his horse and wagon was on Canal Street, passing Orchard Street. When going in the same direction, we usually hitched a ride with him, but if he was going in a different direction, we would just get close to look at the horse and tell Pa Wright hello.

"Dan, we never go to that store, why?" I asked.

Dan said, "Because Daddy doesn't have an account there, so that's why we go to the Raymond's store. Mr. Jesse is really nice too, and I go in there sometimes. His store is hooked onto his house. We will go in there on the way back if he is open, okay? But right now, we get to hurry and get to Mr. Raymond's store and get Momma her BC powder and coke. So come on, soldier, let's pick up the pace."

As we approach Mr. Raymond's store, we could see some big boys out there on the corner looking at us. Dan said, "Terry, get on this side of me and don't say nothing to them, do you hear me?"

"I hear you, but I got some rocks in my pocket. I'm not scared of them. I'm a Bullock," I said before Dan could cut me off.

"Be quiet! Don't say nothing, okay!"

As we walked, I looked up at Dan. He was staring at them, looking from one to the other, and he was not afraid of them either. There were three of them, two of them looked just alike. I would find out later that they were twins and all three were brothers. We went on pass them and inside Mr. Raymond's store. When we walked into the store, Mr. Raymond was behind the counter and looked up as we walked inside.

"Hey, Dan and Terry, how you boys doing today?"

Dan said, "We are doing fine, Mr. Raymond. My momma wants us to get her a box of BC powder and a coke, and we want a pound of cheese, and $.25 of gingersnaps cookies. We're gonna pay for all of it today."

As Mr. Raymond cut the cheese, I saw that he was looking out the window at those big boys, so I started to watch them too. And they were looking into the window, trying to see what we were buying. They were not going to take our stuff from us. Dan said they were mean and might try to take our stuff or ask us for money. I checked my pockets for my big railroad routes as I watched him. I have seven left—three in my left pocket and four in my right pocket—and I know if I hit one in the handle face, it would hurt because I can throw straight and on. As Dan paid Mr. Raymond, he gave me the bag of cookies and cheese. He kept a coke bottle in the bag and put Momma's BC powder in his pocket. I heard Mr. Raymond say, "You boys be careful. Them some mean boys out there. Watch them, Dan."

Dan said, "Yes, sir, Mr. Raymond. Come on, Terry, and stay my right side over here."

Dan put his hand on my shoulder and placed me between him and the store as we watched the two biggest boys converge upon us. I put the bag of cookies in my left hand and got a rock out of my right pocket, gripped it for a hot straight throw, just as one of the boys said, "What you got in that bag, Dan?"

Dan said, "Just stuff. My momma sent us. We not messing with y'all, so leave us alone. Come on, Terry, let's go home."

The big head boy reached for the bag with the coke in it, and Dan snatched his hand back so fast and attempted to swing at his head but stopped short, giving him a warning. "Don't try to mess with us. Leave us alone. I'm not going to tell you again."

The big head boy reached out and tried to grab Dan's arm with his right hand while reaching for the bag with his left hand, leaving his behavior expose as Dan hit him in the here with the bottle inside the bag, causing him to yell out in pain, and said, "Come on, Little Bit," looking at the smaller one who looked just like Big Head, and the smaller of the three came at me in a slow motion sort of way. As I pulled out a rock, I had my hand on as I cocked back to throw the rock as hard as I could; he started to retreat with his arms up above his head to ward off any potential rocks that I might throw at his head, yelling to the others that I had some rocks. Just then, the two big ole boys rush to Dan and swing at him at the same time. Dan was swing in his left hand really fast, and the bottle in the bag with his right hand, keeping himself between me and the boys. The smaller of the boys was looking at the other two, so I stepped around and threw a rock as hard as I could and hit the big head boy right on the side of his head; he yelled out in pain and raced at me. I poured another rock out of my pocket, and as he got close to me, I hit his arm because he put his arms up to ward off the blow. He kept on coming, and he hit me on the head with his fist, and I fell back on the dirt as he snatched my bag of cookies and cheese, tearing my bag and spilling cookies on the ground. Dan ran over and hit him again on the head with the bottle just as I heard Mr. Raymond say, "Hey! You boys, stop that! Leave them alone right now and get away from here, always starting trouble. I'm gonna tell your mama when I see her. Go ahead and leave. Get off my property."

All three of them started walking off down Persimmons Street toward School Street, where Dan said they lived.

Mr. Raymond asked Dan if we were all right. Dan said, "Yes, sir, Mr. Raymond, but can we have two more bags?"

Mr. Raymond said, "Sure, I'll get them for you," disappearing into the store and returning with two more bags, handing them to Dan.

Dan said, "Thanks, Mr. Raymond."

Dan helped me pick up the cookies, and I noticed his lip was busted, swollen, and bleeding a little. "Dan, you let that big head boy hit your mouth. I hit him with two rocks. One time I hit him on the head too," I said with excitement.

Dan said, "They won't bother us no more. They won't fight me one-on-one either. I had to fight so I could keep my eyes on you too. Lois would kill me if anything happened to you, but you did good. You a Bullock, Terry. That is your first combat tour of duty, soldier!"

I said, "Dan, I wasn't scared even, and when I get big like you, I am going to beat up a big year for. You just wait and see me do it, hitting me on my head."

"Come on, we better hurry home, and don't tell Mama what happened. We don't want to worry her and make her head hurt any worse than it does, okay?"

"Okay," I said, touching the side of my head and rubbing it.

Dan smiled at Terry with pride and glad and knot on his head near the hairline so that it is not so noticeable with all that hair.

As we came up to Canal Street, we saw Ms. Viola coming out of Mr. Jesse's store with a big bag in her hand; she was born with little tiny feet and wore the prettiest colorful shoes.

She was the best dressed woman in Little Washington, maybe in all of Goldsboro. She was light-skinned, slim, tall, elegant, and incredibly beautiful.

As we got closer to Ms. Viola, she turned around, waiting and looking at us with a smile, reaching into the bag, finally she said, "Dan, you and Terry, come here. I got a candy bar for you both. Look at him with all that curly hair. How is your mama doing? Tell her I ain't seen her in a while. Tell her I said hello. Here is a Baby Ruth for you Terry, and one for you too, Dan."

Taking the candy bar, Dan said, "Thank you, Ms. Viola, and I will tell Mama you ask about her too. Terry, say thanks to Ms. Viola."

I said, "Thanks, Ms. Viola."

As we began to walk and open out candy bars, Dan said, "Come on before Aunt Leatha comes out and see us because we won't ever get back home fast enough, and Mama's head is hurting."

Aunt Leatha and Momma both looked alike, only Momma was the youngest and prettiest. I don't remember seeing great grandmama before; her name was Pinky Floyd, married to English Floyd; they had two girls and one boy, Jatha Bud Floyd. My other grandmama on my daddy side was Jesse Bullock. Daddy said she lives in Fair Bluff, somewhere close to South Carolina.

As we approached the house, Dan touched my shoulder, cut his head to one side, and I knew he was listening at something, and then he took off into a run, yelling, "Come on," and I took off after him, knowing I couldn't keep up when he ran fast like that. I saw Dan run onto the porch and opened the screen door and went inside. By then, I was close enough to hear Pete and Lois screaming at each other, and I knew they were fighting again. Neither one never really wanted to fight each other, and they never hurt each other. Dan said that they only fought because they were both just alike, just like twins, only Lois was two years older. Both looked very pretty and had strong opinions about everything. Dan said they were just being "Bullocks" and would never hurt each other, and that nobody else better not try to get in between them, or they both would get that person.

I could hear Momma now. "Dan, get between them. Stop them from fighting before they hurt one another. They won't even listen to me, especially Pete."

As I entered the house, I saw that Pete and Lois had each other's hair, and Dan was trying to get their hands apart, saying, "Pete, let go of her hair, and she is going to let go of yours. Y'all got to stop. You both are making Momma's head hurt more than it is, so stop it right now. Y'all better be glad Daddy ain't here. He'll make both of you move out of here. Stop. I said let her go Pete, and she will let you go."

Momma was crying, so I started to cry too. Pete kept yelling and cursing at Lois, and Lois went outside in the back, and Momma went out back too, so I followed. Lois was at the water pump, sprinkling some water over her face.

Momma said, "Girl, I know it ain't just you, but I can't take this. You and Pete need to think about finding somewhere else to go, not right now, but just think about it, and don't worry about the boys. I would take care of them." Lois said, "Terry and Chucky go wherever I go. I ain't leaving my boys here round Daddy, especially Terry. You know he don't like him anyways."

"Girl, he won't bother Terry. You know I will take good care of him," said Momma.

"But Momma, you know how he is when he gets drunk. How he'd beat him the last time. That's why I stabbed him, and I know he ain't forgotten either. So when I go, I'm taking both my boys with me, and I'm going to talk to Coleman today and see if we can stay with him. He lives in a big white house on Center Street, across from the White people, and Ms. Hattie lives there too. I think it's her house, I don't know," Lois said, then she looked at me and said, "Come on, Terry, let me wash your face. You come on with me so we can go talk to Coleman about moving in with him."

I remember telling her that I wanted to stay with Momma, and she said, "I'm your mama, and you're going with me too. So come on, baby, let me wash that dirt off your face. Look at your hair, just as dirty."

I didn't know who Coleman was, but I didn't want to leave my momma, Dan, Tony, Chuck, or Gloria Jean. I didn't know that my young world was beginning to take a turn that would define the rest of my life. However, it would be a long time before we actually moved away.

CHAPTER 5

Cowboys and Indians

The next morning, Dan woke me up, told me to get dressed so we could go outside and get the eggs out of the chicken coop, something we did early most mornings. Once outside, we got to baskets at the end of the porch, and Dan instructed me to start at the other end. Dan would always get the coop that had Big Red in it; she was a fairy me chicken, and it took speed, agility, and nerves to stick your hand inside her domain. She was vicious when it came to protecting her eggs. Big Red was the biggest hen of all; he and we figured Daddy didn't chop her head off and put her in the big cast-iron kettle with boiling water, picked her feathers, cut her up, and let Momma cook her was because Big Red produced the most eggs of all the other hens. Momma would never stick her hands in Big Red's coop because once Big Red scratched her hand and made her hand bleed, leaving a scar, and Daddy vowed to kill her, but Momma took up for Big Red, stating that Big Red was only protecting her unborn chicks. So Daddy let it go, only after saying that if he ever happens again, he'd wring Big Red's neck. So Momma would get Dan to get the eggs from Big Red's coop. If Dan was not around, she would have me to get the eggs out, while she watched and instructed me.

Dan said, "It's going to be hot today. After we get eggs, we're gonna go over to Dion at Hardy's house to play cowboys and Indians. I will let you use my BB rifle, and the rest of us will have bow and arrows. And I want you to listen to me and stay behind me so you won't get shot, okay?"

"But I can't shoot nobody if I be behind you. I might shoot you in the back, Dan," I said.

Dan said, "Don't you worry about that. I will let you know when to shoot at them, okay?"

"Okay," I said.

"All right, you got to be careful 'cause Lois will go crazy if you get pecked or scratched," said Dan.

After we got all the eggs out of the coops, Dan counted a total of twenty-two eggs, and as always, ole Big Red had the most eggs in her coop, which was six. The other has had only three or four eggs in their coops at the most.

Dan said, "We got twenty-two eggs, Terry. Momma would like that this early in the day," said Dan.

As we went into the kitchen, Momma was sitting there, holding her head in her hands and seemed that she always had a headache.

Dan said, "Momma, are you all right?"

"I am fine, just praying. Dan, go in there and wake your sisters up. By the time they get dressed, breakfasts will be ready."

As Dan went to wake up Lois, Pete, and Gloria Jean, Momma got up and started cooking the eggs to go along with our biscuits, grits, and bacon. She then said, "I know you boys want to go out and play, so I'll go on and fix y'all breakfast first, okay?"

"Yes, ma'am."

After breakfast, Dan said, "Come on, Terry, let's go."

And I jumped up and was heading for the door when Lois said, "Go where? Where are you taking him, Dan?"

"We just gonna go over Hardy and Dion's house and play cowboys and Indians. Will be back soon. It's not far. It's on Whitfield Drive," said Dan.

"I know where is at. Don't let him get hurt or too dirty now, okay?" stated Lois.

Dan said, "I won't. You know I always look out for him. Come on, Terry, let's go."

Dan and I started walking down Griffin Street to Dion and Hardy's house. Dan had the big bow and arrows that he made. I had his Daisy BB gun, with two packs of BBs. Dan taught me how to hold the BB gun in my right hand, with it propped up on my shoulder—"like a soldier" he'd say. I still have to use my left hand at times to keep the BB gun in an upright position. It was a nice summer day; the birds were chirping; we had on shorts and T-shirts and no shoes. Each time we took a step, I could feel the powder dirt between my toes. All the streets were dirt streets. We only had to watch out for glass and sharp rocks, maybe a garden snake and dogs that roamed freely. There was hardly ever any traffic; a lot of people did not have cars or trucks where we lived in Little Washington.

The people were coming out to sit on their porches; we knew Aunt Leatha would be on her porch; she always got up real early, just like Momma.

Gloria Jean and I was about the same age and very close to each other, like sister and brother.

"Dan, are we going to go over Aunt Leatha's house to get some of her peach plums?" I asked. "I like them."

Dan said, "We will stop on our way back and get some, but we will stop over her house before we go over to Dion's house to speak, if they are on the porch. Okay?"

When we got to Aunt Leatha's house, when we got closer, Mr. Jesse said, "Where you boys going this early in the day with that bow and BB gun? Hunting?"

"No, sir. We're going over Dion's house to play cowboys and Indians with him and Hardy," said Dan."

"Well you boys better be careful. You know Lois will raise holy hell if something happened to that boy."

Aunt Leatha was in the kitchen when we got there, smiling as always because we knew she made some of the best lemonade around.

"Where have you been, Aunt Leatha?"

She said, "To the A & P store up there on George Street and Ash Street and downtown to the Five and Dime store. They will be back in little while. Y'all come on out on the porch and drink your lemonade," she said while handing us a glass of lemonade. "Dan, you tell Alma I asked about her. Is she still having them bad stomachaches right on?"

Dan said, "She sure is, Aunt Leatha. She needs to go to a doctor and see what's wrong with her head. Daddy said that a new Black doctor from Washington, DC, was going to open an office over by School Street School on Pine Street. I think he said his name was Dr. Hayes. I hope she goes to see that doctor. She wouldn't even go see Dr. Jackson at the drug store on James Street, said it was too far the walk. Maybe Momma will go see Dr. Hayes. Well, we better get going, Terry. Aunt Leatha, thanks for the lemonade. Y'all take care."

"Bye-bye. Y'all be careful, and don't forget to tell Alma I asked about her, Dan, okay?" said Aunt Leatha.

"Okay, I won't forget to tell her, Aunt Leatha," said Dan.

We walked on toward Whitfield Drive with our weapons. Dan with his bow across his chest, with his arrows in his hand with twine tied around them, and I had the BB gun with two packs of BBs in my pocket. I often had to take a few running steps to keep up with Dan because he walked so fast and took longer strides. Sometimes, our cousin Melvin would go with us, but we didn't see him this morning, so we went on without him. He probably went somewhere with our uncle Big June and Aunt Lela. As we walked, Dan was telling me that I was going to be on his side because we are a team, and that Deon and Hardy would be on the same side because they are brothers, like us. When we got the house, Deon and Hardy was waiting for us. Hardy was bigger than Dan; he was a year or two older than Dan, but Dan was bigger than Deon, but about the same height. They both had bows and arrows, with the soda bottle caps at the end (but not on the tips because placing the bottle caps on the end would cause injury) to help the arrow traverse much further, although making the arrow potentially more dangerous. Deon and Hardy went around to the back of the house as we went to the front of the house. The house was a white cinderblock house, with a small stoop and three steps, with bushes lining each side to separate the houses next door, which also could be used to take cover or execute an ambush,

Dan would explain to me. The back and front yards were small, even on the sides, because the houses were closer together, not like ours at home. We could never play over at our house because Momma would go crazy if she knew we were playing cowboys and Indians as we do, with bottle-top tips on the arrows and a BB gun; she would worry that we would get an eye put out as she use to say. She thought we were going hunting for birds and squirrels as we usually did on most Saturday mornings all year-round. However, this day was different… I can vividly remember Dan telling Deon at Hardy that we would be on the same side, and the two of them went to the back of the house as we went around to the front. Dan kept me behind him and told me to watch the corner of the house behind him and to make sure that no one sneaked up alongside the bushes to ambush us. Dan's further instructions were for me to let him know if I saw one of them trying to come up alongside the house or the bushes and to shoot them before they got close. As we took our post, Dan placed all his arrows side-by-side and told me to stay low and not stick my head around the corner. It was then that I heard Dan yell, "We ready when y'all are!"

It became quiet, so much in fact that I could hear the cars and trucks on the truck lane going by. I couldn't see any movement at the rear of the house or alongside of the bushes, so I turned to look at Dan, just as he jumped out to let and arrow fly. And out the corner of my eye, I saw Deon in the bushes, pulling his arrow back from the bow, just as Dan yelled out in pain as he jumped back, and I saw the arrow sticking in his upper left arm, which was bleeding really bad. As Deon lowered his bow and squeezed through the bushes to check on Dan, I pointed the BB gun at his chest and pulled the trigger and cocked the gun, preparing to shoot again, but simultaneously, I heard Dan yelled, "Timeout y'all, I'm hit," as Deon grabbed his forehead and yelled, "Put the BB gun down, Terry. You shot me in my head."

Dan said, "He did right, like I told him. Y'all put the bottle caps at the tip of the arrow, look at my arm."

Hardy said, "Dan, I didn't mean for it to do that. I'm sorry, man."

Dan said, "I know, man. Deon, you okay?"

"Yeah, but tell Terry to stop pointing that BB gun at me. Look at that mean look he is giving me," stated Deon.

"Dan, you want me to shoot him again?" I asked.

"No, let's go home," stated Dan.

Hardy said, "Let me pull the arrow out of your arm, Dan, and put some alcohol on it so it won't get infected."

"No, because it will tear the skin too bad. I will let my daddy take it out, just help me tie a piece of my T-shirt around the top part of my arm to slow the bleeding," stated Dan as he took out his pocketknife and handed it to Hardy. Then holding his tee-shirt with his right hand, he let Hardy cut it all the way around the bottom, then took the piece and tied it real tight, after wrapping it around his arm several times. All of a sudden, without warning, Dan snatched the arrow out of his arm and yelled really loud, then he said, "Hardy, go get the alcohol, man, and something to cover it up for me."

Hardy ran into the house and came back with a white cloth, alcohol, and bandages. When he poured the alcohol on Dan's arm, he grimaced and took the white cloth from Hardy and began to wipe his wound gently and dried his arm off. Hardy began to wrap the gauze bandage around Dan's arm, and Deon took his shirt off and handed it to Dan. Dan took his T-shirt off and put the blue shirt on with Deon's help.

Deon said, "Dan, I'm sorry, man. I didn't know it would do that. I wasn't trying to hurt you, you know that."

"I know you didn't, Deon. Don't worry about it, man. We got to go. Come on, Terry, get those arrows and my bow and hand them to me. We will see y'all later. Don't worry, I will be all right."

We walked home in silence. I could see that the bleeding had stopped. Dan would always get very quiet when he was thinking, upset, or mad about something. He kept wiping the palm of his hand on his upper thighs because his hands always seem to sweat, even more so when something bothered him. He would look down at me and smile every once in a while. That was his way of showing me that he was all right. We didn't stop until we got home. Momma was in the living room with Lois and Pete. When we entered, Momma put her forefinger up to her lips and made that soft sound *sshhhhh* when she wanted us to be absolutely quiet. She then turned the volume dial up on the big wooden box radio, and just then, a White commentator started speaking through the wooden box.

"In the early morning of Sunday, September 15, 1963, Bobby Frank Cherry, Thomas Blanton, Herman Frank Cash, and Robert Chambliss, members of United Klan's of America, a Ku Klux Klan group, planted a box of *dynamite* with a time delay under the steps of the church, near the basement. At about 10:22 a.m., twenty-six children were walking into the basement assembly room to prepare for the *sermon* entitled *The Love That Forgives*, when the bomb exploded. Four girls, Addie Mae Collins (age fourteen), Denise McNair (age eleven), Carole Robertson (age fourteen), and Cynthia Wesley (age fourteen), were killed in the attack, and more than twenty additional people were injured, one of whom was Addie Mae Collins' younger sister, Sarah. The explosion blew a hole in the church's rear wall, destroyed the back steps and all but one stained-glass window, which showed Christ leading a group of little children.

Civil rights activists blamed *George Wallace*, the Governor of Alabama, for creating the climate that led to the killings. Birmingham was a violent city and was nicknamed 'Birmingham' because the city had experienced more than fifty bombings in Black institutions and homes since World War I. Only a week before the bombing, Wallace had told The New York Times that 'to stop integration, Alabama needed a "few first-class funerals."'"

Momma reached over and turned the wooden box radio off, and said, "Lord have mercy, them poor babies. What is this world coming to? I just don't understand how the Lord can let something like this happen to them poor children."

Pete said, "Momma, the Lord ain't had nothing to do with that bombing. That is the devil's work, plain and simple."

"It sure is. Y'all come on and let Momma rest," stated Lois.

So we went back outside and sat on the porch. Lois and Pete went in their rooms. Momma came out and sat in her chair and immediately asked Dan, "Where did you get that shirt, and what is wrong with your arm?"

"We were just playing cowboys and Indians, and I hurt my arm, that's all," stated Dan.

"Come here and let me take a look at your arm, I can… It's been bleeding."

Dan stepped onto the porch, and she reached and gently unwrapped the bandage. When she saw his wound, she said, "Terry, go in the house and look in the medicine cabinet and get that peroxide in the brown bottle, my kit with the bandages in it, and bring it to me."

When I came back, Momma was humming a spiritual song as usual—only this time, I know she was thinking about those young girls that got blown up in that church and mixing spiderwebs and snuff together with her finger. When she saw me, she took the bottle from me and poured some on Dan's wound; he didn't flinch. Momma wiped his wound and started to gently put the mixture of spiderwebs on his wound.

Dan said, "Thanks, Momma. I feel better already."

Momma said, "It ain't as bad as it looks. Here's a Goody powder. Take it. You'll feel better." Ma Simms walked up, and we went on in the backyard. Ma Simms was a big lady and very pretty. She kinda look like Lois. She was a midwife who delivered babies at people houses.

"I didn't know those girls, but I thought of Gloria Jean and Dunkin, and it made me very sad to learn of their demise."

I knew they would be talking about that church bombing as many people did in the coming weeks, months, and years.

CHAPTER 6

Sharpshooting

I remember Daddy coming home because we were around the back of the house on the porch, eating pecans—Tony, Gloria Jean, Dan, and myself. Gloria was trying to get Dan to let her look at his arm and to take the bandage off.

Just as he was doing so, Daddy walked the corner of the house and said, "Dan, let me take a look at your arm?"

As Dan continued to unwrap the bandage, Gloria Jean jumped off the porch in front of Daddy and hugged his waist, always the daddy's girl. As the bandage came off, Daddy stepped closer, inspected the wound, and told Dan to come go with him. Momma came through the back door and said, "Bro, wait a minute, let me put the bandage back on his arm so it won't get infected. And Dan, your daddy is going to take you to see Dr. Hayes so he can look at your arm, but don't worry, it's just a precaution. You probably don't even need sutures, but you might need a tetanus shot. We just want to make sure your arm won't get infected, okay?"

Dan was nodding his head the entire time she was talking to him as always.

When Dan came back, he had a new bandage on his arm. I saw Dan coming back with Daddy when they turned the corner off

School Street. Dan had stopped and was talking to two boys that he went to school with, Lamont and Jason. Daddy just kept right on walking slowly toward home, so I went down Griffin Street to meet him and to go where Dan was until daddy yelled at me, "Get back in that yard right now!"

I turned around and went back to the edge of the yard; as I turned around, I saw Dan had caught up with Daddy. As they approached, I could hear Dan saying, "It was an accident. He didn't mean to do it. We were just playing." Daddy didn't say anything else.

When Dan came up to me, Daddy just kept walking and said, "Tell Alma I'll be over Big Dave's house."

"Yes, sir," said Dan.

"Hey, Dan, what did the doctor do?" I asked.

"He gave me a tetanus shot so it won't get infected and some aspirins for the pain, but it doesn't hurt much at all," stated Dan. "You got any more questions, Einstein?"

"Yeah, why were you talking to those guys while ago?"

"Well, they were asking me what happened to my arm, and Lamont was telling me that they saw ole Tricky Sam on *The Block*, talking to Desi and Dallas doing tricks."

"Who is Tricky Sam, Dan?"

"He is an old man. Don't nobody know how old he is or where he is from. Tricky Sam asked me one time if I had any money in my pockets, and when I told him no, he told me to look in my left pocket, and that I would find a five-dollar bill, so I looked, and it was right there in my left pocket too," stated Dan.

"Is he a magician?"

"I guess he is in a way, but people say he sold his soul to the devil, and that he can give other people money and stuff, but not to himself. That's crazy, huh?"

"Yeah, is he mean, Dan?"

"No, he's always smiling and being nice, but I only saw him two times. A lot of people say nice things about him though, while some people act like he is crazy because they think he sold his soul to the devil," said Dan.

"Dan, come here and tell me what Dr. Hayes did and said to you!" yelled Momma.

So we went up to the front porch, where she was sitting.

Dan said, "Momma, he just gave me a shot and some aspirins and said that you had done a good job with it before I got to him. And Daddy told me to tell you that he went next door to Big Dave's house."

Momma said, "Well, you will be all right. Let me go over there to Big Dave's where your daddy is at. I will be back in a little while. Y'all go on in the backyard and play."

"Yes, Momma. Come on, Terry. Let's go through the house and get the BB gun so we can shoot some cans, soldier," stated Dan. Dan went in the house and got his Daisy BB gun. Gloria was playing with Tony, tickling him, and he was just laughing up a storm. Tony was only three and smart for his age and serious all the time and quiet, just like Dan. However, he was too young to play outside with us.

We went in the backyard to shoot at some cans we saved up. We would sit the cans on the big tree stump in our backyard and take turns shooting them. Dan would always teach me how to shoot the BB gun when he had the time. Dan never seemed to miss, even thought he would stand twenty-feet away and let me stand seven to ten feet away. Dan could cock the BB gun easily. Since I had difficulty, he showed me how to place the butt on my inner thigh for leverage, and then pull the lever up to cock it. This was only after he saw me as I placed the gun on the ground for leverage to cock the lever, telling me that dirt could get inside and damage the gun. This is the same time he taught me about the sight on the end of the barrel and how to place the gun into my right shoulder and just under my chin so that I could learn to aim and shoot properly. Dan always placed five cans on the tree stump and lets me shoot first until I shoot all five cans down to the ground.

"Dan! Dan! Where you at!" screamed Lois. As she approached us, she said, "Boy, who shot you with an arrow that had a bottle cap on the end of it? Let me take this bandage off so I can see how bad that wound is."

"It's not that bad. I already saw Dr. Hayes, and Momma looked at it too," said Dan.

Pete asked, "Did you shoot him back in his arm?"

"No! He wasn't trying to hurt me. He put the top on the bottle to add weight and make the arrow go further, and he said he was sorry," said Dan.

Pete responded by saying, "Sorry my ass. You should've shot him back with this BB gun."

"I had my bow and arrow. Terry had the BB gun," stated Dan.

Lois exploded, "What! Terry was with you? Are you crazy, Dan? He could've gotten hurt too."

"He wasn't going to get hurt. I looked out for him, just like I always do. He was behind me the whole time," Dan said.

While looking at Dan's arm the whole time they were talking, Lois said, "Your arm doesn't look too bad. It's just a superficial wound. Who did it, Dan? And you better tell me too!"

Before Dan could say anything, Terry blurted out, "Girl, Deon shot Dan in his arm with that arrow."

"We still ought to go back round there and beat their asses for shooting him with that bottle top," said Pete.

"He will be all right. They were just playing. Besides, we don't need to worry, Momma."

"Terry, let me see that BB gun?" said Lois.

Terry was holding the BB gun and backed away, cradling the gun to keep it from Lois. As he glanced at Dan, Lois snatched the gun from his grasp. Laughing, she said, "I am going to give it back. I just want to shoot a few cans, okay?" Terry jumped in front of the cans so Lois couldn't shoot the cans. Lois said, "Boy, you better move before I shoot you in your stomach."

"You better not shoot him with that BB gun. Look at him, with his pretty self, looking like Desi Atkinson," stated Pete.

"Move, boy!" Lois screamed. "Before I shoot you now!"

Terry stood there defiantly and said, "No! Give it back. Tell her to give it back, Dan."

Before Dan could react, Lois pulled the trigger and shot Terry right in the stomach; he fell to the ground, holding his stomach, yelling and crying in a painful state of shock, looking up at Lois and wondering how she could hurt him when she was so sweet and kind to him. Seeing the look of concern on her face eased the pain a little as he saw her hand the gun to Dan and started to approach him.

"What is wrong with you? I can't believe you shot him like that," stated Dan.

"Girl, you done lost your damn mind," said Pete.

Lois ignored them both as she rushed to Terry, getting on the ground with him and placing his head in her lap, whispering to him that she was sorry and that he would be okay over and over. Lifting his T-shirt up to inspect his little wound, seeing he had only a little red dot, she said, "Baby, it didn't even break the skin. You are going to be all right. You know I love you. I'm sorry. I won't do that no more, and I won't let nobody else hurt you either, okay?"

As she tried to kiss Terry, he squirmed away from her, trying to act like a big boy, stopped crying, ran over, and snatched the gun from the tree stump, placed the handle on his inner thigh, cocked the gun, and as Lois ran, he aimed at her but never pulled the trigger, and burst out in laughter as she ran screaming.

"Boy, you better not shoot me. Put that gun down, Terry. I mean it too," said Lois, which caused Dan and Pete to burst into laughter.

Dan came over and took the gun from Terry, saying, "What is wrong with you, standing there and letting her shoot you like that? You should've moved out of the way and let her shoot the cans, Pete too, because you know they won't going to be here long, then we could have continued shooting the cans. You a soldier, Terry. Sometimes, you got to retreat so you can fight another day. So don't do that again, okay?"

"Okay, Dan. I won't do it again. Did it hurt you this bad when you got shot with that bottle cap on that arrow?" I asked.

"No, I know yours hurt worst. My wound just look worst," Dan said, looking very serious at Terry.

Lois and Pete had gone into the house. Gloria and Tony came out, and that's when Dan decided to put the gun up and do something safer, he stated, as he headed to the back door.

When Dan came back out of the house, he had a lot of old newspapers under his arm, so I asked, "Dan, what are you going to do with all them newspapers?"

Dan said, "We are going to make a big kite with them, one so big that it will look like an airplane in the sky when we get it up there. We are going to need some more twine and some big reeds, glue, and tape. We are going to hide the papers over here under the house, and we are going to go find some reeds tomorrow. We have everything else we need." Dan removed the bricks from the square opening and placed the newspapers under the house and put the bricks back in our secret hiding place.

We went in the house, and as we approached the front room, we could hear the radio and knew that Momma, Lois, and Pete were listening to something important, because as we came into the room, Lois put her finger up to her lips and whispered for us to be quiet.

Pete said, "Martin Luther King is about to speak at the funeral of the little girls that got killed in that church bombing in Birmingham, Alabama."

Momma was sitting in her chair with Tony on her lap, Gloria was sitting on the corner of the chair, Lois and Pete was standing next to the big wooden box radio, so when Dan went closer to the radio, I went over and sat on the other side of the chair with Momma. When some White man said that Dr. Martin Luther King was approaching the podium, we all got quiet.

Then as his voice came over the radio, he said, "This afternoon we gather in the quiet of this sanctuary to pay our last tribute of respect to these beautiful children of God. They entered the stage of history just a few years ago, and in the brief years that they were privileged to act on this mortal stage, they played their parts exceedingly well. Now the curtain falls. They move through the exit. The drama of their earthly life comes to a close. They are now committed back to that eternity from which they came. These children—unoffending, innocent, and beautiful—were the victims of one of the most vicious and tragic crimes ever perpetrated against humanity. And yet they died nobly. They are the martyred heroines of a holy crusade for freedom and human dignity. And so, this afternoon, in a real sense, they have something to say to each of us in their death. They have something to say to every minister of the gospel who has remained silent behind the safe security of stained-glass windows. They have something to say to every politician [Audience: "Yeah!"] who has fed his constituents with the stale bread of hatred and the spoiled meat of racism. They have something to say to a federal government that has compromised with the undemocratic practices of southern Dixiecrats [Yeah!] and the blatant hypocrisy of right-wing northern Republicans. [Speak!] They have something to say to every Negro [Yeah!] who has passively accepted the evil system of segregation and who has stood on the sidelines in a mighty struggle for justice. They say to each of us, Black and White alike, that we must substitute courage for caution. They say to us that we must be concerned, not merely about who murdered them, but about the system, the way of life, the philosophy which produced the murderers. Their death says to us that we must work passionately and unrelentingly for the realization of the American dream.

"And so my friends, they did not die in vain. [Yeah!] God still has a way of wringing good out of evil. [Oh yes!] And history has proven over and over again that unmerited suffering is redemptive. The innocent blood of these little girls may well serve as a redemptive force [Yeah!] that will bring new light to this dark city. [Yeah!] The holy Scripture says, 'A little child shall lead them.' [Oh yeah!] The death of these little children may lead our whole Southland [Yeah!] from the low road of man's inhumanity to man to the high road of peace and brotherhood. [Yeah! Yes!] These tragic deaths may lead our nation to substitute an aristocracy of character for an aristocracy of color. The spilled blood of these innocent girls may cause the whole citizenry of Birmingham [Yeah!] to transform the negative extremes of a dark past into the positive extremes of a bright future. Indeed, this tragic event may cause the White South to come to terms with its conscience. [Yeah!] And so I stand here to say this afternoon to all assembled here, that in spite of the darkness of this hour [Yeah! Well!], we must not despair. [Yeah! Well!] We must not become bitter [Yeah! That's right!], nor must we harbor the desire to retaliate with violence. No, we must not lose faith in our White brothers. [Yeah!

Yes!] Somehow, we must believe that the most misguided among them can learn to respect the dignity and the worth of all human personality.

"May I now say a word to you, the members of the bereaved families. It is almost impossible to say anything that can console you at this difficult hour and remove the deep clouds of disappointment, which are floating in your mental skies. But I hope you can find a little consolation from the universality of this experience. Death comes to every individual. There is an amazing democracy about death. It is not aristocracy for some of the people, but a democracy for all of the people. Kings die and beggars die, rich men and poor men die, old people die and young people die. Death comes to the innocent, and it comes to the guilty. Death is the irreducible common denominator of all men.

"I hope you can find some consolation from Christianity's affirmation that death is not the end. Death is not a period that ends the great sentence of life, but a comma that punctuates it to more lofty significance. Death is not a blind alley that leads the human race into a state of nothingness, but an open door, which leads man into life eternal. Let this daring faith, this great invincible surmise, be your sustaining power during these trying days.

"Now I say to you in conclusion, life is hard, at times as hard as crucible steel. It has its leak and difficult moments. Like the ever-flowing waters of the river, life has its moments of drought and its moments of flood. [Yeah! Yes!] Like the ever-changing cycle of the seasons, life has the soothing warmth of its summers and the piercing chill of its winters. [Yeah!] And if one will hold on, he will discover that God walks with him [Yeah! Well!), and that God is able [Yeah! Yes!] to lift you from the fatigue of despair to the buoyancy of hope, and transform dark and desolate valleys into sunlit paths of inner peace.

"And so today, you do not walk alone. You gave to this world wonderful children. [Moans.] They didn't live long lives, but they lived meaningful lives. [Well!] Their lives were distressingly small in quantity, but glowingly large in quality. [Yeah!] And no greater tribute can be paid to you as parents, and no greater epitaph can come to them as children than where they died and what they were doing when they died. [Yeah!] They did not die in the dives and dens of Birmingham [Yeah! Well!], nor did they die discussing and listening to filthy jokes. [Yeah!] They died between the sacred walls of the church of God [Yeah! Yes!], and they were discussing the eternal meaning [Yes!] of love. This stands out as a beautiful, beautiful thing for all generations. [Yes!] Shakespeare had Horatio to say some beautiful words as he stood over the dead body of Hamlet. And today, as I stand over the remains of these beautiful, darling girls, I paraphrase the words of Shakespeare: [Yeah! Well!] Good night, sweet princesses. Good night, those who symbolize a new day. [Yeah! Yes!] And may the flight of angels [That's right!] take thee to thy eternal rest. God bless you.'"

(By Dr. Martin Luther King Jr., September 18, 1963, Sixteenth Street Baptist Church, Birmingham, Alabama. Delivered at funeral service for three of the children—Addie Mae Collins, Carol Denise McNair, and Cynthia Diane Wesley—killed in the bombing. AA separate service was held for the fourth victim, Carole Robertson.)

"Momma, are you all right?" Lois asked.

Momma said, "Yeah, I am all right, just thinking about them little girls being killed all because somebody wanted to act devilish and bring misery into the lives of others, all because they want to feel superior and do the devil's work. People are people, and there's good and bad in everybody, no matter who they are. It just doesn't make sense that those little girls had to die like that, and so young. Lord have mercy. Dan, you and Terry go to the store and get me a Goody powder and Coca-Cola. Here's a dollar, and get you and Terry something and bring back some cookies for Gloria Jean and Tony too."

"Okay, Momma. Come on, Terry. Let's go to the store," said Dan.

As we were going out, Pete said, "Them White people are just hateful and full of hatred against Black people, and for them to blow up that church like that with those girls in there just makes me sick to my stomach. Damn Klansmen."

As we got on the dirt road to walk down Griffin Street, I asked Dan, "What is a Klansmen?

Dan said, "Boy, you hear everything. A Klan is an organization of White people that is still living in the past and bent on the destruction of Black people. They are mean and just don't care, but not all White people are like that. Like Momma said, there are good and bad in everybody, no matter who they are. That's what you need to remember."

"Well, why did they put a bomb in that church and blow up those little girls?" I asked.

Dan looked down at Terry and smiled at him and said, "I just told you they want to destroy Black people, and come on, we need to get to the store and get Mama's Goody powder and coke."

As we turned off Griffin Street onto School Street, we saw Jason, so Dan stopped when Jason called out to him.

Jason walked up smiling and saying, "Hey little Desi, you look just like Desi Atkinson, and Lois baby boy look just like Dallas, my daddy."

Dan said, "Jason, don't tell him that. He doesn't know all that yet. And if he tells Lois, she is gonna cuss you out. Where are y'all going at?"

Jason said, "We are going to down to the Sand Hole and swim for a while. It's going to be hot today. Johnny and Eddie are meeting me there. Bernard will come with them too. Are we going with them, or you gonna go down there, Dan?"

"I don't know yet. I might later on," said Dan.

"Jason, here comes Joan with her pretty self," said Lemont.

As we looked, Joan and her little brother Tony was coming off Persimmons Street toward us.

Lemont said, "Here comes Joan and your brother. He is probably Desi's boy too. He is just as yellow as Terry and look just a like."

"Lemont, cut that out and quit jiving man. Come on. Let's go to the store, Terry. I will see y'all later," stated Dan. "Terry, don't ask me if that's your brother because of what Lemont said. He doesn't know that for sure. He's just talking, like always."

As we got closer to Joan and Tony, he said, "Hey, Joan."

Joan said, "Hey, Dan and Terry."

We kept on walking and turned on Persimmons Street, where Mr. Raymond's store was. A lady was raking her yard and spoke to Dan as we passed, and Dan said, "Hey, Mrs. Lewis. That was my second-grade teacher at School Street School. She will be yours too when you get in the second grade. She looks just like Dianna Ross who sings with the Supremes," said Dan.

We went into the store. Mr. Raymond said, "Hey boys, come on in. Nice to see y'all. How are doing today?"

"We are doing fine, Mr. Raymond. Momma wants us to get her a Goody powder and coke, and we want ten commodore cookies since they are a penny a piece, and twenty lemon cookies, and twenty gingersnaps too since they are two for a penny, also twenty-five cents worth of cheese," said Dan.

After getting all that we came for, we left the store and headed back home. As we turned back on School Street, Terry noticed that Dan was not only quiet but had a concerned look on his face, so he asked, "Dan, what's wrong with you?"

Dan looked down at Terry, smiled, and said, "I was just thinking about Momma and how she keeps having a headache all the time. I just hope and pray that she is all right. She worries about everything—Lois, Pete, Daddy, all of us—and now she is worried about those little girls that got killed in that church bombing. And especially since they were the same age as Gloria Jean, and with Lois taking you to church with Rev. Coleman, she just has a lot on her mind. Lois says it is something about it being the time of the month, whatever that means. Come on, let's speed up. Momma is waiting on us to get back home. Let's eat some of these cookies before we get home because we got to make our kite. It's already windy, and Momma said a hurricane is coming. She's always listening to the weather on the radio."

Once we got back in the house, we could hear Sam Cooke singing from the radio:

> Darling you send me,
> Honest you do, honest you do, whoooaaa
> ooohhhh

At first I thought it was infatuation
But it's lasted soooo long
And now I find myself wanting
To marry you and take you home

I know I know I know, you send me
I know you, send me
Oooohhhhh, you, you, you, you honest you do
Honest you do

Mama was just smiling with her eyes closed, moving her head, sitting in her favorite rocking chair, humming to the song; she liked Sam Cooke, and so did everyone else.

Momma always seemed to be humming a song, gospel, blues, or soul.

"Momma, we're back, and I got your Goody powder and coke," said Dan.

"Thank you, child. I feel better already. You and Terry go on outside and give Gloria Jean and Tony some of those cookies and cheese. Let me have a few for Chucky. He likes them too, even though he doesn't have any teeth yet," Momma said while smiling down at Chucky in her lap. Momma was always playing with his hair because it was like black silk (as she used to say).

CHAPTER 7

Flying High

Gloria Jean and Tony was in the backyard, sitting on the porch when we went out the back door and looked up when they heard us. Dan jumped down on the ground and placed the two bags of cookies on the porch. He took one bag and tore it carefully down the middle and did the same to the other bag. Dan then took out his pocket knife out his cut-off jean short's pocket and took the cheese and cut it up in small squares, placing them on the open paper bag as we all watched. He placed a piece of cheese on a gingersnap and handed it to Tony, and then fixed one for Gloria Jean, then me, and after he fixed one for himself, he said, "Gloria, now you can fix yours and Tony. Terry can fix his own. Come on, Terry, let's get the newspaper and reeds so we can put our kite together".

Dan laid out the reeds, making a cross, and tied the twine at the intersection. Dan would explain to me what he was doing and why, mainly to keep me out of his way. Dan said, "First, we got to put these two reeds together and make sure they are even like this. Terry, come here, hold these two pieces so I can tie them together. Now, I'm going to tie this twine all the way around each point, then glue the paper over it."

Once we got the kite put together, Dan took the old sheet that he got from Momma, put the end in his mouth, and pulled on it hard, tearing the sheet and pulling it all the way down to the end, repeating this action until he had eight pieces. He took four pieces and tied them together and added the other four pieces at the end of the first four pieces to make the tail longer because the kite was so big, bigger than ever before. "Terry, this kite is going to fly really high just like a plane, you will see," said Dan.

I asked, "How do you know that, Dan?"

"Because the wind is already blowing hard, and if it's blowing hard down here, I know it's blowing even harder up in the sky. That's why we're we put a long heavy tail on it. Plus, our kite is really big and will be able to fly in strong winds too. You'll see. Trust me," said Dan.

"Dan, I always trust you, you know that," I said.

Dan laughed and said, "I know."

Gloria Jean came around the corner of the house and said, "Dan, Daddy said for you and Terry to cover up those chicken coops." Gloria then darted back into the house.

Dan went to the side of the house and got the tarps and dragged them out, separating them. "Come on, Terry, hold this end while I lift this end over the top and drag it over the coops," stated Dan.

We did the same to the other end of the coops, and just as we finished, we heard Lois. "Dan, you and Terry better get in this house right now!" screamed Lois. "Don't y'all see that lightning and hear all that thunder? That hurricane Cleo is getting closer. Momma heard it on the radio, and it might even be some tornadoes with it too, so y'all come on in the house right now! Come on!" Lois waited on us too.

Dan said, "Let's go inside, Terry. I'll put this kite in the hallway because we can't fly it in the rain. It will get wet and then crash. Plus, the winds will be too strong. Come on, let's go. She is waiting on us."

When we went inside, everyone was standing or sitting around Daddy; he was holding Gloria Jean in his lap; she appeared to be asleep as he was talking. Momma was holding Tony in her lap. Lois and Pete were sitting on the sofa, listening intently.

Daddy was saying, "Them hurricanes form off the coast of Africa at the same places the slaves got on them ships to be brought over here to be sold on auction blocks like animals. Many of the slaves died from starvation, pneumonia, and when they got weak from rowing, they were thrown from the ships into the sea, not to mention the ones that were killed out of meanness and, worst of all, the raping and torturing of the women and young girls on them ships. It's just a damn shame. I believe that the same path them boats took is the same path them hurricanes take, following them angry tortured souls. Yeah, following the same path with all them bones laying down there on the bottom of all that water, thousands and thousands of miles of bones scattered from Africa to North and South America, England, Ireland, and Lord only knows where else. It's just a damn shame, I tell you! I believe that's why Black folks got high blood pressure right now today, suffering from being separated from their families, some sold and tricked by their own tribes, thinking they going to a better place. On them slave ships, subjected to the pain, trauma, being beat and whipped, raped and killed like animals. And every time I hear that damn song, *Amazing Grace,* it makes me sick to my stomach ever since I learned a White captain on a slave ship wrote it. And Black folk singing that dreadful song just turns my damn stomach. I guess people can change, but it ain't right for people to do the work of the devil and then expect God to forgive them, but that's how works. I tell you, some things just don't sit right with me. Then we get over here and continue to go through hell, from the year 1619 until to this damn day. Slavery hurt us Black folks down to our spirits and our blood for all generations to come. Them White people can pass all the laws they want, but most White people will never ever see us Black folks as equals. A man is a man, born with a silver spoon or not. The Bible say a man will earn his living by the sweat of his brow, and that means by working, like I do. must really hurt them to know Jesse Owens and now Bob Hayes are the fastest men to ever run on this earth, and there ain't no White man who could whup Sonny Liston, and I know Cassius Clay ain't gonna let no White man whup him in no boxing ring. Beat that British champion up really bad from what I heard. Now, that boy can box for real. That boy be talking junk too"—laughing—"even told Sonny what round he was gonna knock him out in, talking bout he floats like a butterfly and sting like a bee. Yeah, we all human beings. There's good and bad in everybody, and when a man works and take care of his family, then he is a man." Then he was quiet for what seemed an eternity, so was everyone else. Then Daddy broke the silence, "Dan, come on and go with me. We need to go out here and check to make sure that everything is tied down and covered up. Don't want nothing flying through the windows or to lose the crop or any of the chickens. This is going to be a bad hurricane this time. It's got to be with a name like Cleo," he said, laughing.

"Yes, sir," said Dan.

We always gather around Momma when there was a storm and listen to her hum. She would always have us to be quiet as the thunder and lightning would start. Momma would always hum a song, and she could hum so beautifully, along with the sound of the rain hitting the tin roof. As Momma hummed, we could hear the rain on our tin roof and hear the wind outside blowing harder and harder. The louder the rain got and the harder the wind blew, Momma still hummed at the same level and tone, calming us all; it seems she even calmed the rain and wind at times. We didn't get to go back outside that day. I hardly ever remember going to bed, just waking up in bed. I do know that Momma or Lois would always put me in bed.

The next morning, when I was awoke, I could hear the radio on; and when I went into the front room, everyone was in there, except Daddy; he was gone to work. The commentator was saying, "A tropical wave that exited the coast of Africa on August 15, 1964, moved westward, not organizing into a tropical depression until around 890 miles (1432.3 km) east of *Barbados* on August 20 as reported by a navy reconnaissance plane. It continued west north-westward, quickly strengthening to a hurricane the next day with a minimum central pressure of 993 *mb*.

"Early in the afternoon of August 22, Cleo crossed *Guadeloupe* as a 115 mph (185 km/h) category 3 hurricane. The hurricane continued to strengthen as it moved through the Caribbean Sea and reached its peak intensity of 155 mph (250 km/h) on the August

23 while south of the *Dominican Republic*. It maintained that intensity for a day, bringing heavy rain and winds to *Hispaniola*. As Cleo passed south of *Haiti* on August 24, it veered northward momentarily, enough to move on to the Southwest Peninsula of Haiti. The circulation of the hurricane was greatly disrupted by the mountainous terrain of the island, quickly weakening the hurricane.

"Cleo weakened to a category 1 hurricane before hitting southern *Cuba* on the August 26. It crossed the island quickly. Shortly after emerging from the north coast of Cuba, Cleo restrengthened to a hurricane, having weakened to a tropical storm while over Cuba. Cleo managed to intensify to a 100 mph (160 km/h) category 2 hurricane before hitting the Miami, Florida (http://www.ask.com/wiki/Miami,_Florida?qsrc=3044) area on August 27. It weakened to a tropical storm while over *Florida* on the twenty-eighth. The center moved offshore between *Jacksonville* and *St. Augustine, Florida,* before moving back onshore near *Savannah, Georgia* on August 29, without any increase in intensity. Its northward path along the Florida coast was unusual for the month of August.

Cleo continued to weaken as it moved through the Carolinas, drifting through as a tropical depression. After bringing heavy rain through the area, Cleo exited into the Atlantic Ocean, near *Norfolk, Virginia*, and quickly intensified to a tropical storm again on the September 1."

Pete said, "That White man just said that Cleo exited off the coast of Africa, just like Daddy said."

As Momma turned the radio off, Lois said, "Pete, that's because Africa is always hot and near the equator."

"You both might be right so stop trying to argue. Y'all just gonna get Momma upset. You know she always got a headache. We don't need to be worrying her," said Dan.

Momma came into the room and said, "Leave them be, Dan. You and Terry come on and go outside with me so we can check on the chickens and the garden."

When we went outside, Momma said, "Dan, go on over there and check on them chickens and take that tarp off them cages, get the eggs out if you see any, and take the broken ones out too and throw them away in the trash barrel, Baby."

She got a basket off the corner of the porch. "Terry, you come on with me and help me get this corn off the ground and put them in this basket." After collecting the corn, filling the basket up, she said, "Baby, go get the garden hoe for me so I can drain some of this water off these crops."

Terry quickly went to get the garden hoe; as he was coming back, he heard Momma scream loud and saw her jump back, pointing at the ground in front of her. "Baby, take that hoe and chop that snake up. Get it!"

Terry raised the garden hoe over his head and swung down with all his might, striking the snake in the middle of his body, cutting it in half, raising the garden hoe over his head again and again, chopping the snake into little pieces, until Dan rushed over and stopped him.

Reaching for the garden hoe while laughing, Dan said, "Terry, that's enough. You killed him. He's not even poisonous. It's just a garden snake."

Momma said, "I don't care what kind it was. All of them can still bite, and Terry, baby, you just killed the worst enemy in this world. They are all serpents, poisonous or not. I can't stand no snakes."

When we finished the yard, Dan went in and brought the kite outside. It looked bigger than when we first made it. As we prepared to set flight, Dan laid out three big balls of twine and explained to me that as the kite got higher and higher in the sky, we have to tie another ball of twine to the first one so that the kite could go even higher. Dan let the kite out about ten feet, then started backing up at a fast pace as the kite started to lift into the air like a real airplane. Dan stopped going backward and just let twine unroll, and the kite just kept going up. The higher the kite went up, the smaller it got. The kite looked magnificent as it waved around in the sky, becoming smaller and smaller.

Dan said with excitement, "I told you that I could get this kite to fly really high. Look at it soar like a real airplane. It's way up there too. Come over here and hold this part with me so you can feel the strength and power it has against the wind."

"Wow! I can really feel it too, Dan."

Each time Dan would pull down on the twine, a few seconds later, the kite would waver way up in the sky. I could not believe how small the kite was or how high it was in the sky. The exhilaration was as high as the kite. We were flying high… People started to come out and watch. Norman and his little brother Alvin came through the backyard. They lived behind us in front of the railroad tracks. Dan's friend Jason and Lamont came over, along with several others, to see our kite fly high.

"Dan, how did you get that kite way up there in the sky like that. Man, we followed that kite all the way over here. You can see it over by School Street School, even over on Carolina Street," stated Jason.

As Dan moved me over so he could reach the third ball of twine, he then handed me the twine and said, "Terry, hold this right here"— pointing about twelve inches from the end of the twine—"real tight so I can tie this twine on the end. Jason, I made this kite, and Terry helped me too. I am going to make it go even higher. You just watch me."

When Dan finished tying the twine, he took the kite from me and started to unwind the roll of twine as he pulled down on it. As he backed up a few steps, he said, "Did y'all see that? Watch how I make it wave in the wind."

Lamont said, "Dan, that ain't no regular kite. It got to be really big for it to be that high, and we can still see it. The clouds are rolling by fast, and that kite is way up there in the clouds. It looks like one of those planes going to Seymour Johnson Air Force Base."

It was then that Dan exploded, "Oh man, it broke. The twine just broke. Look at it going down. It is going to crash and break up. I'm going to go get it. Terry, you stay here in the yard. Come on, y'all…"

Dan, Norman, Lamont, and Jason took off running toward the backyard, going through Norman's yard, across the tracks, and toward Elm Street until I couldn't see them anymore. When I went in the house, I could hear the song "Loco Motion" by Little Eva. (*Everybody's doing a brand-new dance now. Come on, baby, do the loco motion. I know you'll get to like it if you give it a chance now. Come on, baby, do the loco motion…*). As I entered the living room, Momma was sitting in her chair, smiling and rocking to the beat.

She said, "Terry, do you know that my momma, Pinky Floyd, is from Kinston, North Carolina, and that Little Eva is from Kinston too. She might be my cousin. I don't know though. Anyway, where is Dan?"

I said, "He went to find that kite. It broke and was flying by itself in the wind. He told me to stay in the yard, so I came in here with you."

"Well, when he gets back, I want y'all to go to the Green Parrot and get me a cheeseburger and some fries. I like one of those cheese-burgers every once in a while. I think they have the best in Goldsboro. You and Dan can get one too." Chuck started to cry, and Momma got up to get him; as soon as she picked him up, he stop crying and started smiling and seemed to be dancing in her arms, so Momma just started swaying and singing along with the song as I went back outside.

(*There's never been a dance that's so easy to do. It even makes you happy when you're feeling blue. Come on, baby, do the loco motion …*)

CHAPTER 8

The Block

When Dan came back home, he was alone and did not have the kite with him. Even though it was windy, he was sweating profusely. He went straight to the water pump and started pumping the handle with one hand while pouring water from the bucket into the opening of the pump in order to prime the pump. Dan pumped vigorously, and in seconds, the water began to gush. He placed his head under the pump and continued to pump as he drenched himself. As Dan stood up, he pumped water into the bucket and began to drink the water in gulps. He then walked over to the tree stump and sat down, smiling at me.

I asked, "Why you so tired drinking all that water like that?"

"I ran all the way over by the Playboy Club on Elm & Center Street, went over those railroad tracks in that big field, and all the way over to George Street and still couldn't find that kite. I believe it landed on Kemp Manufacturing Company's roof or on the roof of those buildings behind the Playboy Club. On the way back, I went on The Block, so I just came back home. I saw Sissy. She asked about you, and the little one name Blanche too," Dan said while laughing.

"Dan, I like Sissy. She is pretty and got long pretty hair."

"She is my age, just short," Dan said. "She is too old for you. The little one name Blanche is your age."

"Well, I like Sissy, not her. Why you always laughing at me when I tell you I like Sissy? She likes me too, Dunkin likes me, and Glory Jean likes me too, but you don't laugh about them," stated Terry.

Dan said, "That's different. They're family, but Sissy ain't no kin to us, and anyway, when you get big, a lot of girls are going to like you 'cause you're a Bullock and you got curly hair, not to mention you're yellow too," Dan said while laughing.

Terry seemed to be in deep thought, squinting his eyes while looking at Dan. Then he said, "Dan, Momma wants you to go on The Block and get all of us some cheeseburgers from the Green Parrot. Momma said I can go with you too."

"Okay, but it's a lot of water out there, on Pine Street, School Street, and especially on George Street because of Hurricane Cleo. A lot of areas are flooded, so we will have to take our sneakers off when we get to George Street, then put them back on after we get through the water. If it's too deep, I will let you get on my back, and I will take you across. Let's see what Momma wants, okay?" Dan jumped on to the back porch as I took the steps.

As we entered the house, we could hear Sam Cooke's music playing. (*It's just another Saturday night, and I ain't got nobody. I got some money 'cause I just got paid. Now, how I wish I had someone to talk too, I'm in an awful way*). Momma was sitting in her chair, rocking Chucky in her lap. Gloria was playing jack rocks on the floor as Tony watched.

"Momma, Terry said you want us to go to the Green Parrot."

"I sure do. I want you and Terry to go up there to the Green Parrot and get nine hotdogs and two cheeseburgers. Cheeseburgers don't cost nothing but fifty cents, then go across the street to the sandwich shop and get two smoke sausage sandwiches. Here, take this five-dollar bill. You get three hotdogs for a dollar, the cheeseburgers are fifty cents, smoke sausages are a quarter, and on your way back, stop and get me a BC powder and a coke. I got a stomachache. It's Saturday, and I don't feel like cooking. And if you see Lois and

Porter, tell them I said to come home. And don't let Terry walk in no water. Glass and sharp rocks can be under that water where you can't see it."

"Yes, ma'am. I will look out for him. I know how Lois is about him. He will be all right, and I will tell them you said to come home too, Momma. Come on, Terry, let's go to The Block."

"Dan, are we going by the Grill?" I asked.

"No, we are going to go up on Elm Street, and if we don't see Lois and Pete on The Block, we will come back on Pine Street and see if they are in the Grill, but they are probably over Doris's house or at Willie's poolroom. Don't worry, we will find them," said Dan. "We got to hurry back and stop at Dr. Jackson's drug store and get Momma a BC powder and a coke so her head will stop hurting. It's across the street from the Green Parrot."

"Dan, Momma don't act like her stomach be hurting. She always smiling and humming to the songs that come on the radio," I said.

Dan said, "Well, that's because she doesn't want us to worry about her. I hope that nothing is wrong with her. She needs to go see Dr. Hayes. That's what Daddy keeps telling her, so does Lois and Pete too. She prays all the time, so she will be all right. Come on, let's walk faster like soldiers. Hup one-two-three, hup one-two-three, hup one-two-three. Let's get up this hill, and we will be on James Street. It's Saturday, so a lot of people will be up here on The Block. We might see your daddy Desi. If we do, he will give you some money like he always do, then we can get some green ice cream in The Green Parrot."

I said, "But Dan, his last name ain't like mine. He got another last name. We are Bullocks. He is something else."

"Yeah, his last name is Atkinson," said Dan. "So you got two daddies, and they both love you. We all love you. That's all that matters. Look, I told you a lot of people are out here on The Block. I see Big Dave over there, shining shoes. I see Desi's blue Mack Truck over there in front of his liquor house. He is standing outside, talking to Mr. Dallas and Mr. Earl. We can go over there, but let's go over here to Doris's house first and see if Lois and Pete are in there."

As we walked up to the house, we could hear people talking and laughing, so we walked up to the porch and knocked on the screen door, and Doris said, "Come on in here, Dan and Terry. Lois and Pete are in the need of your money, and we don't know you."

The old man said, "Son, everybody calls me Tricky Sam."

Before he could say anything further, a loud voice beside us said, "You heard what kitchen. Lois, Terry, and Dan are in here. Come here, Terry and Dan, and give me a hug. Dan, you are growing up so fast, just as tall as me, and look at you, Terry, looking like Uncle Desi with your pretty self."

I said, "Girls are pretty, so I ain't pretty."

Lois, walking through the door, said, "You are pretty, and you my honey boy, come here. What are you and Dan doing up here? Is Momma all right?"

Dan said, "She wants you and Pete to come home. She got a headache, and she want y'all to come take care of Tony and Chuck. She doesn't feel good, and she told us to go to the Green Parrot and get some food because she doesn't feel like cooking, and we got to get her a BC powder and a coke for her headache."

Lois said, "Pete, come on, we better get back home. Momma ain't feeling too good."

Pete said, "Girl, I heard what Dan said. Look, Dan, you and Terry go on and get the food Momma told you to get, her BC powder and coke, and come back over here, and we will be ready to go, okay?"

Dan said, "Okay, come on, Terry, let's go."

And as we were leaving, Ralph, Jack, Man, Wheata and Whitley (the twins) were coming into the yard, and the oldest one, Ralph, was asking if we were coming back, and Dan said, "Yeah, but to get Lois and Pete because we had to get back home because Momma had a headache and we had to eat, so we can't stay this time."

Ralph said, "Okay, Dan. Look at Terry looking like his daddy, Uncle Desi, over there on the corner. You know he wants to see him, Dan."

"I know, when we come back from the Green Parrot and get Lois and Pete, she will take him over there to see him. Come on, Terry," said Dan.

As we approached the front of the house, people were everywhere, and some were still in their shiny cars; everyone seemed happy and dressed up all nice, and as we approached the Green Parrot, there was crowd around a man; he was very dark and old, his eyes were red, and his voice was deep.

Dan said, "Terry, here comes your daddy," just as the old man reached for my ear and touched it, I pulled back. He was handing me a brand-new shiny Kennedy fifty-cent piece, but Dan swiftly stuck his hand out as the old man tried to hand me the money, blocking his hand, and said, "Sir, we don't, Dan said, and don't ever try to touch my son again, or do no tricks on him, do you understand me Sam?" said Desi.

The man just nodded his head and walked off toward Willie's poolroom. A few people followed him, while others went in different directions.

"Dan, what are you and Terry doing up here?" asked Desi.

"We came up here to get Momma a BC powder and coke and some food from the Green Parrot and to tell Lois and Pete to come home. They are over to Doris's house, and when we finish, we got to go and get them so we can go home. What was that man's name, and how did he pull that fifty cent out of Terry's ear like that?" asked Dan.

"That was Tricky Sam. He doesn't mean no harm. They say he sold his soul to the devil, and that he can do tricks and tell the future among other things, but don't you worry about him, he won't bother you or Terry again," said Desi.

"Will you drive us home when we get ready to go?" asked Dan.

"Sure, I will. I'll be over Doris's when you get finished. How are you doing, Terry? You get bigger and bigger every time I see you. Here is a dollar, and one for you too, Dan," stated Desi, reaching into his pocket, pulling out a wad of money.

"I told you he would give us some money. Now we can buy some green ice cream and even get some chocolate sodas too and have money left for tomorrow," said Dan as he opened the door to The Green Parrot. "Terry, that's Dot and Mr. Al. They own the Green Parrot, just like Mr. Jones owns the sandwich shop, and Dr. Jackson owns the drug store, and Willie owns the Poolroom, and your Daddy owns the Liquor House over there too. One day, we gonna own something up here on The Block."

"How we gonna do that, Dan? We ain't got no money like them," I said.

"Well, that's right, for right now. Because when I go into the war and come back home, I will have the money to open my own business, and we can run it together and make a lot of money so we can take care of Momma and our whole family. Here comes Dot. Let's give her our order so we can get out of here," said Dan.

"Hey, Dan and Terry. How y'all doing today?" Before we could even answer, Dot hit us with a barrage of questions. "Dan, you sure getting taller, and you too, Terry. What brings you two up here today? Where is Lois at? Do Desi know that Terry is up here? Lord, let me stop asking so many questions. I am just glad to see you both, that's all. You ready to order?" Taking out her pad, she said, "Now what do you want, Dan?"

After Dan gave our order and finished eating our green ice cream, we had Dot to put the bags into a small box. We went across the street to the drug store. Rev. Artis Coleman was on his way out and held the door open for us, asking if we've seen Lois.

Dan said, "Yes, she is over to Doris's house. I will tell her you asked about her," said Dan.

"Okay, well, may the good Lord watch over you and your family, especially the little one there. His name is Terry, I believe. God bless you, son. Be sure to tell her I asked about her, Dan," said Reverend Coleman.

"Hey there, Dan, it's been a while since I last saw you. You getting to be as tall as Bro Bullock. How is Alma doing? You tell Alma I said hello, and I will try to get down there to visit her when I can. I see you got little Desi with you. What's his name? Terry?" asked Evelyn.

Dan said, "Yeah, that's his name, Ms. Evelyn. I need to get Momma a coke and a BC powder for her stomachache. I should get her more than one. She seems to keep a stomachache these days. Let me get five of them, please. How much will that cost, Ms. Evelyn?" asked Dan.

"I want you to tell your momma to come in and see Dr. Jackson about those stomachaches or go to Dr. Hayes. Tell her I don't care where or which Doctor she goes to, just go to one or the other. I'm not going to charge you anything for the coke or the BC powder, and you tell her that I'm praying that she will be just fine and for her to go see a doctor," said Evelyn.

"Yes, ma'am, and thank you very much, Ms. Evelyn. I will let Momma know that you didn't charge us for the medicine or the coke. Where is Ms. Dot at? Is she working today?" asked Dan.

"Oh yeah, but she got Earl to take her to pay some bills. She will be back later. I will let her know that you asked about her. She will hate she didn't get to see you and Terry. Come on. Y'all want to have some ice cream with me?" asked Evelyn.

Dan said, "No, ma'am. We just ate some of that green ice cream at the Green Parrot. Sorry about that. I just wanted Terry to try it for himself since he never had any before."

Just then, an old man came in with a cane; he was bent over, with a hump in his back.

"Hey, Mr. Tappin, how are you today?" asked Evelyn.

Mr. Tappin looked around and said, "How you are doing, Evelyn? I came to pick up my medicine. How are you boys doing?"

Dan said, "We are doing good, Mr. Tappin."

Evelyn said, "Mr. Tappin, that's Bro Bullock's boy, and the little one is Desi's boy. That's Dan Bullock and Terry Bullock."

"I know. The little one looks just like Desi. There's something special about you boys. I just don't know what it is. You boys stay out of trouble and remember the golden rule, 'Do unto others as you would have them do unto you,' and it will carry you a long way," said Mr. Tappin.

"That's right," echoed Evelyn.

"Dan, what's wrong with that man, all bent over like that?" I asked.

"I don't know. I guess he was born that way. People say that if anybody disrespects him, they will have bad luck. But like Momma always say, we have to respect our elders, even if we don't agree with them. He did give us some good advice, with that golden rule, 'Do unto others as you would have them do unto you.' We have to treat people the way we want people to treat us. It's only right, according to God. Hey, let's see how Big Dave is doing. Look at him, shinning them shoes, popping that rag." Laughed Dan.

Just as Big Dave was finishing shinning, he turned around with that big smile, and said, "Hey, Dan and Terry. What you boys doing up here? I saw you both go over to the Green Parrot a while ago. Whatcha got good to eat in that box for me?"

Dan said, "Momma sent me to get this for the family. She doesn't feel like cooking. She got a stomachache. Momma still having them stomachaches. Come around and see her. I'll will be glad when Bud Floyd comes back home. He comes around a lot."

Big Dave said, "Dan, when are you going to come and let me show you how to shine shoes so you can put some money in your pockets?"

"I will have to ask Daddy, but I know he is going to say no because I have to stay near Momma so I can help her out, especially with Lois and Pete going to work. Anyway, it was nice seeing you. We got to be going now. Come on, Terry, and let's go get Lois and Pete so we can hurry and get back home," said Dan.

As we approached Doris's house, Lois and Pete were coming out with Desi, and Lois said, "We were just coming to get you and Terry, so Desi can give us a ride home. Where have y'all been at? Y'all been gone for thirty minutes?"

Dan said, "We were talking to Evelyn in the drug store and then Big Dave. We saw old Tricky Sam. He pulled a Kennedy fifty-cent piece out of Terry's ear, but Desi made him give it back, and then gave us a dollar. One time, Tricky Sam put a five-dollar bill in my pocket."

"You stay away from that devil and keep Terry away from him too. I don't want y'all talking to him, do you understand me?"

Pete said, "We need to tell him to stay away from them!"

Desi said, "I told him to stay away from them, so you don't have to worry about him no more. Come on so I can get y'all home. The truck is over here. Dan, you and my boy get on the back. I won't drive too fast."

As Lois and Pete got in the cab of the truck with Desi, Dan put the box in the bed of the truck and helped me get inside. As we drove off and got to Elm Street, Tom and Leroy came out of Hamilton Funeral Home and waved at Desi. Tom walked up to the truck and was talking to Desi, and Desi handed him some money out of the window.

As we turned the corner, Dan said, "Desi loaned him some money, and Tom got to pay him back 50 percent on each dollar. He makes a lot of money that way, but I am going to go in the army and make my money as soon as I get old enough to sign up. You just wait and see."

I said, "Hey, Dan, I am going to go in the army when I get big enough to go in too."

Dan seems to be in deep thought as usual, always thinking about going into the army, so I just shut up. As we turned onto Griffin Street and pulled up to the house, Dan jumped off the back of the truck as soon as it stopped rolling and reached to help me get off, then got the box, and we went inside, leaving Lois and Pete outside talking to Desi.

As we walked off, Desi said, "Bye, son. Dan, tell your Momma I said hello."

"All right, I will," said Dan.

As we went into the house, Momma was sitting in her chair, listening to the radio and turned it off as we came into the room. "Dan, where's the coke and BC powder? My stomach is killing me, son. Give everyone two of those hotdogs to Gloria Jean, Tony, Chuck and Greg, and you and Terry get two, bring me one of those cheeseburgers, and Lois and Pete can get theirs when they come inside. There's some lemonade in the refrigerator. Pour them some in a glass," said Momma, just as Lois and Pete walked into the house.

"Here, Momma. Desi gave me twenty dollars to give to you and for me to tell you hello. I told him I was going to marry Reverend Coleman. He doesn't believe me, but I am," said Lois.

"Girl, that man is way too old for you, and you are way too young for that man," Momma said.

Pete said, "I am going to get married to get Reverend Coleman to marry me and Jean too. I want my own house."

"I know you both got your minds made, so we will see what happens. All I can do is pray and let the Lord have his will. I don't know what Bro will have to say about it 'cause ain't neither one of you old enough to get married unless he says so. Go on in the kitchen and get yourselves a cheeseburger or hot dog and some of that lemonade. I need to rest now, so watch them babies and make sure they eat. I got to nurse this stomachache, child."

Pete said, "Momma, you need to go see Dr. Hayes about that headache you keep having all the time. That ain't right. I know you be praying, but God gave some people the power to heal, like doctors, so you need to go on and see Dr. Hayes before it gets even worse. You ain't supposed to be hurting all the time, and those BC powders and cokes don't seem to be working at all."

"Well, I can't argue with that, and I am thinking about seeing Dr. Hayes. Go in the kitchen and eat, and don't be worrying about me. I will be all right," said Momma.

We went on the back porch and sat while we ate our hotdogs and drank lemonade, and Dan said, "I sure hope Momma go and see Dr. Hayes. It seems like her stomachaches are getting worse and worse every day. Lois and Pete in there talking about getting married and moving away. It's like our family are going to change and split up, and we got to stay a family, and we gonna stay a family no matter if they do get married and move away. We will still see each other and spend time together, so Terry, don't worry about nothing. I will always be there for you. When I go in the army, I will come back, or you will come in the army where I am, so we will still be together, ain't that right?"

I said, "Yep, we sure will, Dan, because we are family."

Just then, we heard Lois singing off the top of her head from the kitchen, "I've been through it all, to what seems like hell and back, with no one to even call on. All by myself, and so, so alone. Lord, the pain and loneliness, I would hide, you see. Things so, so bad. I call on Jesus. Lord, have mercy on me."

Then Pete joined in with her soulful voice, singing off the top of her head, "Everything I do, Lord, seems to turn out so, so wrong. My days are nights, and my nights are days. I feel so, so weak, Lord, and just no longer strong. I cry, Jesus. Lord, have mercy on me." Then they started laughing.

Dan said, "I can't tell which one sound the best. They sound just alike to me, both sound good… While one sang, the other always hummed along, and together, they would just make up their own songs and always enjoy singing together. Although two years apart, they were almost like twins and inseparable. That's how we are going to be when we get older, Terry, inseparable."

"What does that mean, Dan, inseparable?" I asked.

Dan put his hands on Terry's head, looking him straight in the eyes, and said, "It means no matter what happens, or where we are, we will still be brothers, and we will be together, even if we are not together, and we will still be Bullocks, and we will still be family. Nobody can change that, so I want you to always remember that. Don't never ever forget, okay?"

"I won't never forget, Dan," I said.

MY MEMORIES OF THE YOUNGEST AMERICAN HERO, PFC DAN BULLOCK

MOTHER
ALMA FLOYD BULLOCK
SEPT 23   JULY 17
1920   1965

Purple Heart Banquet, August 6, 2022

My lawyer, Tommy Jarrette

CHAPTER 9

Family in Crisis

The next morning, Momma was in the kitchen, talking to Lois, Pete, and Dan as I walked in, and she was saying, "God love us so good that he wouldn't let us know when or what time we would leave this earth. I've been thinking about them young children down there in Alabama that got blown up in that church, lives taken way too soon. I just know that they are in heaven with the Lord now, but can you imagine if the parents would have known those children would have left this earth so soon? It would have been pure torment for them. I pray day and night that the Lord will keep his hedge around all my children and grandchildren, in fact, all children, and just bless and protect all of y'all. I can't help but worry. That's probably why my stomach hurt all the time."

Lois said, "Momma, you need to stop worrying so much. We are going to be all right. It was the devil that put them White people up to bombing that church. God ain't have nothing to do with that, and you know it."

"Girl, I know that. I worry because I don't know how long it will be before I leave this earth, and I can't help but imagine that it won't be much longer. I just don't know when it will be, but I got a feeling it won't be long," said Momma.

Pete said, "Momma, you always talk like that lately, saying the same thing over and over. It not only depresses you, but it depresses us too. Look at Dan and Terry standing there looking at you, and Dan looking like he about to cry, and if he start, you know Terry is going to start crying too. You are going to be just fine. You need to go see Dr. Hayes so he can figure out what's going on with your stomach. We know you ain't pregnant." Pete started laughing.

Momma said, "That ain't even funny, and I know that I say the same things over and over at times, because as I get older, my thought process tends to grow a little weary, even cause me to question my own ability to remember. I guess that's why I say some of the same things over and over, or ask the same questions over and over, especially when I feel and believe it is important to me or to whomever I am talking to. And it's almost always the people I love the most, like Bro and my children and grandchildren, that I ask the same things over because I want to make sure I did say it, because it is important to me. So if I ask you something that I have already asked you, please just answer me again without any malice, and when I tell you something that I already told you, just pay attention and know that I am just trying to make sure that I have told you what I wanted you to know because it has to be important to me for me to ask over and over and important for y'all to know. And if any of you see that I am weak in an area, then I need you to be strong for me, not mock me or think less of me. I didn't think less of any of you or mock you when I had to change your diapers and feed you." Smiling. "I am not getting any younger. And I know that you all are worried about me, and I will go see Dr. Hayes. It's gotten to point where a coke and BC powder don't seem to help me much anymore."

"Momma, you know ain't nobody mocking you. We all love you, and we're so happy that you are going to see Dr. Hayes. I know that Daddy will be glad to hear that when he comes home," said Lois.

"Momma, you know I will always be strong for you, and I will go with you to see Dr. Hayes too. All of us can go with you, Momma, you know that," said Dan.

"Yeah, I know that, but your daddy will take an off so he can go with me. We will be going to see Dr. Hayes in the morning. Dan, you and Terry go to the store and get me a coke and BC powder and get a few packs of Kool-Aid and some cookies, mix them up, but before you go, go out there and get those eggs out of the coop and bring them in here so I can start breakfast," said Momma.

Dan said, "Yes, ma'am. Come on, Terry. Let's get the eggs for Momma. I will get the ones out of Big Red's coop. She always has the most, so you start on the other end. Get your basket. Hurry up so we can go, okay?"

After only a few minutes, we had gone through the six coops and gathered up eighteen eggs, took them into the kitchen, and gave them to Momma.

"Come on, Terry. Let's go to Mr. Jessie's store this time. Besides, he is just as close since we went to Mr. Raymond's store the last time. I like Mr. Jessie. His last name is English, like it came from England, or maybe England is called that because the people who founded England spoke English. I asked Mr. Jessie about his last name, but he always say he doesn't know, then he always asks me where our name originated from. Then he asks me about our last name, and I tell him that our last name is a surname, an Indian name, from the Croatan Tribe, but I heard Daddy say that it's the name of the male oxen, or a young bull, a chosen name to represent our family and how strong we are and how strong our bloodline is too. But my teacher said that the name Bullock was originated in England or somewhere overseas but does agree that it is a surname and originally named after a bull or male oxen. So either way, it is our name, and it means that we are strong, Nathan Terry Bullock," Dan said while holding up both arms and making a muscle in each arm, looking at me laughing.

As we walked down Orchard Street and approached Canal Street, Pa Wright was riding by on his horse and wagon.

"How you boys doing today? Get on the back, and I will give you a ride," said Pa Wright.

Dan said, "Sir, we are just going to Mr. Jesse's store, and we got to get back home. Maybe the next time."

Pa Wright said, "All right, tell Bro and Alma I said hello, and your sisters too." Then Pa Wright turned around and hit the reins and said, "Giddy-up," and the horse started to walk at a slow pace, just as he always did.

Just as we were about to go into Mr. Jesse's store, Aunt Leatha called out to Dan and said, "Dan, when you and Terry finish over there, come over here. I got something for you to take back to Alma, okay?"

Dan said, "Yes, ma'am," as we watched her go back in the house.

As we entered the store, Mr. Jesse was sitting behind the counter, talking to Ms. Viola. Ms. Viola was a pretty lady; she looked almost white, always dressed very elegant every day, and her little shoes always matched her clothes. Her feet were very small and turned inward (some people say she was born that way), yet she seems to have no problem with her gait. As soon as she saw us, she said, "How you handsome young men doing. Look at you, Dan, just as tall as I am. You are growing up so fast, and look at you, Terry, with all that curly hair, just as cute as a button. Both of you, come and give me a hug." Dan stepped forward and gave her a hug, then she stepped over to Terry, who was shying away, and said, "Come here, with your pretty self, looking like your daddy." She hugged Terry and kissed his forehead. As Terry wiped his forehead, frowning up as he did so, Mr. Jesse started laughing with that big bellowing voice. Mr. Jesse was a big man, standing at six-four and weighing almost three hundred pounds, just a jolly ole fellow.

"Viola, leave my customers alone and stop hugging and kissing everybody that comes in my store. You gon' run my most valued customers away, and you know how Lois is about that boy. Look at how he is looking at you," Mr. Jesse said.

Viola said, "Jesse, let them get a soda and some of them cookies and put it on my tab, and that goes for anytime they come in here, okay?"

"I sure will, and you boys tell her thank you. She is just as sweet as she can be," said Mr. Jesse.

Terry was the first to say, "Thank you," and then surprising everyone, especially Ms. Viola, by walking up to Ms. Viola and reaching out his arms to give her a hug.

"Aaah, that's so sweet. Thank you, sweetheart. You just made my day, honey," Ms. Viola said while hugging Terry. "Well, let me get out of here. I'll see you later, Jesse. Dan, tell Alma I said hello and keep me in prayer, and I will do the same, and your sisters too. All right now, y'all boys be good," said Ms. Viola.

"Okay, Viola, see you later and have a blessed day. Dan, how can I help you and Terry. What kind of soda and cookies you and Terry want?" asked Mr. Jesse.

"Well, Terry can only have chocolate sodas, and I want a grape soda, and we want some gingersnap cookies. Then I want to get a BC powder and a Coca-Cola for Momma, and we need some paper bags so we can go pick some pecans. Do you want some when we pick them? We sell them for a quarter, but we will give you a bag of pecans for free because you are giving us the bags, and you are always nice to us," said Dan.

Mr. Jesse turned to the drink box and got the two sodas out, and coming back to the cash register, he said, "Terry, here's your soda. Let me get a bag so I can get your cookies, and you can have a few of these medium-sized bags, and I will take a rain check on the pecans. Here you go, son. I gave you ten cents worth. That's thirty cookies, so you can share with the others when you get home," all the while handing Terry a bag of cookies. All right, Dan. Here you are, son," handing Dan the grape soda and bag of cookies, along with the coke and BC powder. "Now you boys take care and tell everybody I said hello. Dan, you are growing so fast. Before long, you'll be as big as I am," said Mr. Jesse with that big booming laugh again as we walked out of the store.

"Hey, Dan, I like Ms. Viola. She is really nice, and she said we can get what we want from Mr. Jesse's store, and he can put it on her tab," I said.

Dan said, "Yeah, she is really nice, but not just because she bought us sodas and cookies, and we don't have to get something every time we come to Mr. Jesse's store just so he can put it on her tab. That will be taking advantage of her and her kindness. We are Bullocks, so we don't, and can't, take another person kindness for weakness. Remember the golden rule, 'Do unto others as you will have them so unto you.' Do you remember Mr. Tappin telling us that, and Momma always tell us the same thing?"

"Yeah, I know. Old man Reverend Coleman told me the same thing too. Dan, Lois is going to marry Reverend Coleman. He is a preacher in the church, and we are going to go stay with him in a big white house somewhere, but I don't want to go. I'm gonna stay with Momma," I said.

Dan said, "You are going to have to go, but don't you worry, I will still get to see you all the time, and you can still come and stay with Momma on the weekends, and you will still go to School Street School. You will just be sleeping over there, that's all. Reverend Coleman is a man of God, and he is a good man. Everybody likes him. He doesn't curse, drink liquor, or smoke cigarettes. It will be good for you and Chuck to go stay with him and good for Lois too. Pete is getting married too. She is going to marry Jean White because I heard her and Lois talking about it, so she is going to move and take Tony and Greg with her. Me and Gloria will stay with Momma and Daddy. That's what happens when people get older, and you know Daddy stay on Lois and Pete, and they are tired of him and want to leave, and they don't want to worry Momma anymore. That might be why Momma's stomach be hurting. Just don't you worry. Everything will turn our just fine. Come and let's see what Aunt Leatha want."

As we walked up the steps, Aunt Leatha came to the door with a big bag and handed it to Dan and said, "Hey, Dan, take these collards to Alma. I told her I was going to give her some as soon as they got big enough, and how is she doing? Is her stomach still giving her trouble?"

"Yeah, Aunt Leatha, but she is going to go see Dr. Hayes in the morning. Daddy is going to go with her. He's taking and off from work, so she is going to be all right. We need to get back so I can get her this coke and her BC powder, and I will tell her what you said. Come on, Terry, let's go home. Bye, Aunt Leatha," said Dan.

"Well, go on. Don't forget to tell her what I said, and tell her that I love her too. Dan, I heard that Lois is going to marry Rev. Artis Coleman. She knows that man is way too old for her. Well, you boys be good."

"Yes, ma'am," said Dan.

"Hey, Dan, is Momma gonna be all right? Everybody knows about her stomach, and they really like her and keep asking us how she is doing. I know why everybody likes Momma, because she is the sweetest person in the whole wide world," stated Terry.

Dan looked down at Terry and saw how serious he looked and just smiled, knowing how much he loves family and because of how he seems to feel things deeper than most people, even older ones too. That's why Momma says he wears his heart and emotions on his sleeve.

As we entered the house from the back door, into the kitchen, as we usually did, Gloria, Tony, Chuck, and Greg were at the kitchen table, still eating breakfast, and Momma came into the kitchen.

Dan said, "Momma, here's your BC powder and coke. And Aunt Leatha sent you these collards, and she asked how you were doing, so did Mr. Jesse and Ms. Viola. They all said they were praying for you to get better and was happy to hear that you were going to see Dr. Hayes in the morning too. Ms. Viola bought me and Terry a soda and some cookies for everybody."

Momma said, "Viola is a good woman, like an angel. She will give you the clothes off her back. You can't talk about her without speaking of angels. That's why the Holy Bible tells us to be aware of strangers, for many have entertained angels, unawares. Most people who are born with a physical challenge are kind of mean and walk around upset at the world sometimes, but you won't ever see Viola upset or seeming to have a bad day. I could use all the prayers I can get, especially from Viola. Gloria, get them up and put those plates in the sink. I will wash them out later. Wipe that table off. Dan, you and Terry sit down. It won't take me a minute to fry these eggs. The grits are still warm and the sausage is too," said Momma.

After we ate, we went outside, just as Lois and Pete was leaving, and Dan asked them where they were going, and Lois said, "We'll be back. I got to go see Coleman and get the key from him so I can get Desi to move us. We are moving to a nice big white house on the corner of Pine Street and Center Street. Pete is going to move to Lagrange. Just look after Terry and Tony. Gloria will help Momma with Chuck and Gregory. We'll be back. We are not moving until next week, and you and Gloria will be able to come visit us anytime you want too."

Pete said, "Dan, we will bring back some hotdogs for everybody from the Green Parrot when we come back. Keep your eyes on Tony. You know how he tries to follow you and Terry, okay?"

"Okay. If we go back to the store, he can go with us. I will look out for him."

Once they started walking down Griffin Street, Dan said, "Come on, Tony, you can go with me and Terry. We are going to go pick some pecans."

Tony was a quiet and serious boy and mature for his age. He just smiled and nodded his head. Surprisingly, Tony said, "Dan, Pete said we are going to be leaving and staying in another house, and I can't stay with Momma no more, and I don't want to go. Greg and Chuck don't want to go either. Why we got to move away?"

Dan put his hand on Tony's shoulder and said, "Tony, just like I told Terry, you will still see Momma, Daddy, Gloria, and me all the time. It will only be like you are sleeping in another house. You will still come back home all the time. I will come to see you too and bring Gloria with me too. So don't you worry. Everything is going to be just fine. Come on, let's go over to School Street, by the school. There are some big pecan trees over there. Maybe Ms. Lane will buy them. She always gives me fifty cents for a bag, and she is always nice too, and she love to talk. Mr. Ed, he just smiles a lot. He doesn't talk too much."

After picking up five bags of pecans, we walked over to Mr. Ed Lane's store, and Mr. Ed was a White man, but he was very well-liked and always nice to everyone, so was his wife, Ms. Mary.

As we walked in, Ms. Mary said, "How you young gentlemen doing today? I hope those are pecans in those bags. I was wondering when you were going to bring me some more, Dan. I don't know why you charge a quarter, but like always, I will give you fifty cents for each bag? Hey, Terry, look at you, head full of curly hair. It gets longer and longer every time I see you, and you get taller and taller.

You catch up with Dan before too long. Who's the little one, just as cute as a button?"

Dan said, "Hey, Ms. Mary and Mr. Ed, this is my nephew, Tony. My sister Pete's son."

Ms. Lane said, "Oh my Lord, he looks just like her. I should've known. Sugar, what kind of cookies do you like to eat? Commadores, gingersnaps, or butter cookies? Since it's your first time, you get some free cookies, just like all the rest of the kids. So what kind would you like, Tony?"

Tony looked at Dan, and Dan nodded his head up and down, and Tony said, "I like gingersnap cookies. Thank you, Ms. Lane."

"You are so very welcome, sugar, and just as well-mannered as Dan. You are some good boys. How many bags do you have, Dan? Five? That's two dollars and fifty-cents. Ed, give Dan two dollars and fifty-cents, while I get Tony some gingersnap cookies," said Ms. Lane.

After Dan got the money and Tony got his cookies and hugs from Ms. Lane, we left out and started on our way back home. Tony gave us a cookie as we walked, stating that he would give Momma, Gloria, Chuck, and Greg a cookie too.

As soon as we turned on Griffin Street, we knew that something was wrong. The ambulance was in front of our house, and Dan took off running, and Tony and I ran, trying to keep up, but Dan was much faster, so we started to walk. As we approached, Momma was sitting on the porch, and the rescue personnel was walking back to the ambulance, and Pete was telling them that Momma needed to go to the hospital. Lois was telling Pete to calm sown because Pete was eight months pregnant and didn't need to be upset, that she was going to call a cab to take Momma to the hospital. As Lois walked off, Dan said, "Pete, why didn't they take Momma in the ambulance to the hospital?"

Pete looked at Dan and said, "Because they don't care, and because she is Black, talking about because she is sitting up, it's not an emergency, and it might just be indigestion. We told them that she has been hurting for months, but they wouldn't listen to us. It ain't right," said Pete.

Lois went across the street to use the phone, to call a cab. People were outside, looking and saying that they should have taken her to the hospital. Dan and Pete were on either side of her, holding Momma's hand, and she started to hum a spiritual song as she always did to calm herself and those around her. Dan went inside and came back out with a BC powder and a coke and handed it to Momma, saying, "Momma, take this BC powder and drink some of this coke. Maybe it will you until the cab comes and take you to the hospital."

Momma took it and drank some of the soda, then said, "Dan, thank you. Don't you worry. I will be alright. Go in the house and get my shoes for me and take care of everybody while I am gone. I will be back. Lois and Pete can go with me to the hospital. Let your daddy know where I am when he comes home. Tell him I will be just fine and not to worry. I might be back before he gets home anyway," said Momma.

Lois came back and said, "The cab is on its way. Pete, I will go with her. You need to stay home and get off your feet."

"Girl, I am going too. I am all right. Dan will take care of the children," said Pete.

The cab was going really fast as he pulled up, in a cloud of dust. Lois and Pete got on each side of Momma and held her by the arms and gently guided her to the cab as Dan opened the back door so they could help Momma get in the back seat. Porter went around to the other side and got inside, while Lois got in the front seat. We all stood around and watched the cab take off, then Dan told us all to come in the house. Tony gave Gloria, Chuck, and Greg some cookies. Dan was quiet, and we all followed suit, then Dan said, "Everybody, bow your heads and let's pray. Lord Jesus, please let Momma be all right and make her well so she won't hurt no more and can come back home. We pray in the name of Jesus Christ, amen."

We were all outside in the backyard when Lois came out on the back porch and said, "We are back. Momma is resting, so I want all of you to be quiet when you come in the house. Her doctor wasn't there, and Momma has to go see him on Monday. They want her to have an enema, so stay out here while me and Pete give her an enema, then I will fix something to eat for everybody, so be good and don't worry, okay?" Then she went back inside.

Everyone still looking at the door, then we all looked at Dan. Gloria started walking toward the door, and Dan stopped her, put his arms around her, and said, "Gloria, Momma is going to be all right. Let's stay out here like Lois told us too. Come on, let's sit on the porch, so I can tell y'all about some of our family. On Daddy's side, we got a granddaddy, and his name is Dan Bullock too. I was named after him, and grandmomma's name is Jessy Bullock. They live almost in South Carolina, in a town called Fair Bluff. Daddy got about three brothers. He is the oldest, then there is Luther, Theoscar, and George. There are some sisters too: Marie, Inez, and Alberta. Lois and Pete met them and their children too. Marie has a daughter named Michelle and a son named Ralph. I was a baby when I went there. I don't remember them. When I'll get older and get a car, I will take y'all down there to meet them. Momma's momma is Pinky Floyd, and her husband is Amos. Momma has a sister, Leatha, and two brothers: Luther and Bud. We know all of them because they live here in Goldsboro, and Uncle Bud because he comes around all the time. Momma is the youngest one of them all and the prettiest one too." Dan laughed, and we all started to laugh, just because he was laughing. Dan didn't laugh too often ever since Momma started to complain about her stomach. He was always serious and quiet, but lately, he was that way more than ever. Everyone noticed it because they would always tell him not to worry or ask him if he was all right. He would always smile and tell them that he was okay or doing just fine.

"Dan, come on inside and bring everybody with you. Momma wants to talk to y'all because she doesn't want us to worry about her and want you to know that she is gonna be just fine. So, come on, I'm going to go help Lois in the kitchen before she messes up the dumplings. We are cooking some chicken and dumplings and some of those collards Aunt Leatha sent around here. Don't be making no noise and asking too many questions. She needs her rest," said Pete.

Dan said, "All right, come on, let's be quiet."

As we went in the house, we could hear the music playing in the radio, and Pete was singing and dancing along with the music, by the Supremes, rubbing her pregnant stomach:

Baby love, my baby love
I need your ya, ohhh how I need your love
I need ya, baby, baby I need you

Momma said, "Pete, turn that music down and quit singing so loud so they can hear me when I talk. Thank you," said Momma as we walked into the room.

We all went in the room, and Momma looked good; she said, "Well, I went to the hospital, and Dr. Miller wasn't there, and he won't be back before Monday. I will go back to the hospital on Monday and see him then. They just told me to have an enema, something that will help to clean me out, and Lois and Pete helped me with that. I called y'all in here because I don't want y'all to be worrying about me because I will be all right. Terry, come here. You stop crying. I told you I will be alright. You are going to always wear your heart on your sleeve. I want y'all to go on in the kitchen and eat. Lois is calling y'all. Go wash your hands and face. Dan, you and Gloria make sure you wash Chuck and Greg's face and hands. Dan, when you finish eating, I might want you to go to the store for me if Bro doesn't stop by there and get me a coke and BC powder."

Dan said, "Yes, ma'am. Momma, I have money, and I wanted to go to the store anyway. I took Tony and Terry with me, and we went and picked up five bags of pecans. Ms. Mary gave me fifty cents for each bag, so I will buy you a coke and BC powder. Plus, we need some Kool-Aid and sugar. So can we go to the store when we finish eating?"

"Sure. You can take Tony and Terry with you. Don't y'all be trying to eat all fast either. Take your time," said Momma.

"Momma, we're getting ready to go. We ate all our food," said Dan.

"Okay, turn the radio back up before you go and be safe. Go straight there and come back," said Momma.

Dan walked over and turned the radio up, and Momma started smiling when she heard "The Four Tops." She started moving her head from side to side. (*Sugar pie, honeybunch, you know that I love you. I can't help myself. I love you and nobody else. In and out my life, come and you go, leaving just your picture behind, and I kissed it a thousand times. When you snap your finger, or wink your eye, I come running to you...*).

We could still hear the song as we were leaving the yard. Terry and Tony were trying to sing and dance; everybody likes that song.

"Come on, Momma said for us to hurry back. Hup one, hup two, hup three. Come on, soldiers. Let's move it. Hup one, hup two, hup three. All right, men, repeat after me, 'Move it on cross the railroad track..." Terry and Tony, repeating after Dan, moved it on across the railroad track. "Hey, ladies, we're back."

"Hey, ladies, we're back."

"Hup one, hup two, hup three. Hup one, two, three."

Sometimes we would march halfway or all the way to the store, but since Tony was with us, Dan went slower, and we stopped after three quarters of a block and walked the rest of the way to Mr. Raymond's store since it was closest. Mr. Raymond was always nice and always had on his clean white apron.

"How you young men doing today? Who is this little man, looking like Pete?"

"We are doing all right, Mr. Raymond, and that's Tony, Pete's son. He does look like her," said Dan.

"What can I do for you gentleman this afternoon?" asked Mr. Raymond.

Dan said, "Well, first of all, I need to get a two BC powders and two cokes. I want a twenty-five cent worth of cheese, and twenty-five cents of gingersnaps, twenty-five cents of commadores, and twenty-five cents of chocolate chips too. Also, five packs of grape Kool-Aid."

"Well, Dan, that will be one dollar and eighty cents unless you want me to put it on the tab, son," Mr. Raymond stated as he was counting and putting the cookies in the bag. "Would you like anything else, Dan?"

"No, sir, Mr. Raymond, and I will pay for it now. We sold five bags of pecans today for twenty-five cents a bag. Let me know when you want some too. If you give me the bags, I will give you a discount, okay?"

"Oh yeah. What kind of discount, Dan?" asked Mr. Raymond.

Dan said, "Maybe I will charge you twenty cents a bag. The bags are medium-sized, but if you give me extra bags, I will only charge you fifteen cents. So what do you think, Mr. Raymond?"

Mr. Raymond turned around from wrapping the cheese and said, "Dan, I think you are going to a very successful businessman when you grow up, and I don't even have to give it any thought. I will give you all the bags you need and will take the fifteen-cent discount. Although I'd only want a bag or two. Maybe each week for pecan pies. Is that all right?"

"Yes, sir, that's all right, but Mr. Raymond, I am not going to be no businessman. I am going to be a soldier in the army. I will make sure I bring you at least two bags of pecans tomorrow, if nothing doesn't happen," said Dan.

We gathered up the bags and the things that we had bought. Dan handed Tony a bag and gave me one, and we headed back home.

As soon as we turned onto Griffin Street, Dan said, "See that car, I think that's Reverend Pate's black car. He must have brought Reverend Coleman over to pick Lois up because he doesn't drive, and he doesn't have a car. See, I told you. She is waiting for you, Terry. She got Chuck with her."

Lois was looking down the street at us, holding Chuck by the hand, standing next to the car.

"Dan, is she waiting for me?" I asked.

"I guess so, but I will talk to her so you can stay with us, so don't you worry."

Once we got close enough, Lois said, "Terry, do you want to stay with Dan? I am going to take Chuck with me because Momma don't need to be bothered. I must go to our new home and straighten it out. I will be back tomorrow when I get off work. I will get Desi to bring me over here to get you, okay? So you be good, and Dan, watch out for him. Come on, Chuck, get in the car, baby." As she opened the car door, Chuck tried to pull away and started to cry because he didn't want to leave Terry.

Terry went over to Chuck, hugged him, and said, "Chuck, I am going to come with you tomorrow, and we will still be able to come back over here to see Glory Jean, Momma, Tony, and Greg too, so don't cry."

Lois and Chuck got into the black shiny car. Reverend Coleman waved at us, and so did Reverend Pate as they drove off down the dusty dirt road. We stood there watching the car move off in a small cloud of dust.

Momma was sitting in the living room, talking to Pete when we walked in.

Momma said, "Dan, open that coke for me and give me that BC powder, and I want y'all to sit down and listen to me because I know y'all got questions. Terry, you and Chuckie are going to live with Lois, and Tony, you and Greg are going to go live with Pete. But y'all can come see me anytime you want too and even spend the night on weekends and come by after school since the school is so close. So don't y'all get upset or worried. Everything is going to be just fine. Now y'all go on out back and play. Pete is going to make y'all some Kool-Aid to go with all of them cookies and cheese. Tomorrow is Sunday. Lois will be back to get you this evening, or tomorrow, Terry. I must go to the hospital so I can get well. So won't nobody be here because Pete will be moving tomorrow too. I will be back, and I will send Dan to get you so you can come and spend the weekend with us, so don't you worry. The weekend will be here before you know it."

The next day, after saying our goodbyes, Pete and Jean White loaded up his truck, and Tony and Greg got inside and left. Tony wanted to stay but had to leave. Momma seemed so sad, standing in the doorway. It was getting dark when Desi pulled up in his blue Mack Truck. Lois got out and came inside and was talking to Momma, and when I went in the living room, she said, "Hey, honey boy, you about ready to go. Come give me a hug."

I said, "I want to stay with Momma."

"I know you do. I do too, but we got to move, and you will see her all the time. Dan and Gloria too. I will bring you back to see, and you can spend weekends with her too. Dan and Gloria will come and see you, even walk you back over here sometimes. It's not that far, just around the corner from The Block, on the corner of Elm Street and Center Street. We will be upstairs, Sweet and Betty lives downstairs, and they have children that you know and can play with. So come on, we need to get going. Give Momma, Dan, and Gloria a hug," said Lois.

When the weekend came, I was outside playing with Chuck, and he called out Dan's name, and I looked up and saw Dan waking toward us. So we walked up to him, and he looked worried, like he had been crying too.

"Dan, what's wrong?" I asked.

Dan said, "Has Lois come home from work yet?"

"Not yet," replied to Terry.

Dan said, "Momma is still in the hospital. Maybe that's where Lois and Pete are at. I had to walk Gloria Jean over to Aunt Leatha's house. I walked her over there so I could come up here with y'all. I will stay until Lois come back. Where is Reverend Coleman?"

"He's gone to paint somebody's house, but Ms. Sweet is looking out for us, and Ms. Betty too. But now you are here, so we are all right. How come Momma is still at the hospital? I thought she was back at home," I said.

Dan said, "Well, Daddy said she had an operation, and they are keeping her in the hospital until she is well enough to come home, then he left. I don't know where he went but said he won't be back for a while. He was with that lady named Jewel. I don't know who she is, but he said something about New York, so maybe she is from there, but he acted like he had known her for a long time. I don't know what's going on with our family. Pete and Lois getting married and moving away, and Momma still in the hospital. Daddy told me and Gloria to go stay with Aunt Leatha until Momma come back home, like he ain't gonna be there at all, or go to work. And it's been weeks since we last saw him. But you know what, we just got to pray more, just like Momma always say."

"Hey, Dan, you gon' got bigger than when I last saw you. Lois told me your momma was in the hospital. My prayers are with her. Have you eaten anything? Are you hungry?" asked Sweet.

Dan said, "She's still in the hospital. She had an operation, and she will be back home soon. I already ate though. Thanks anyway."

Sweet said, "I already gave Terry and Chuck a hotdog and some lemonade. Well, if y'all need anything, just let me know. I will be in the house."

We went inside when it started to get dark. Dan turned the radio on, and it was talking about Rev. Martin Luther King, and Dan turned the radio up louder. The South-African broadcasting network has accused the Rev. Martin King Jr. of being violence-orientated and a communist sympathizer. It was apparently an official reaction to a proposal by the South-African Nation Students' Organization to invite the American Negro civil rights leader to South Africa for a series of lectures. A commentator on the network's daily current affairs program. Dan turned the radio off as we heard Reverend Coleman coming up the stairs. We could tell it was him because of the heavy slow footsteps. Lois footsteps were faster and much lighter; she was much younger than Reverend Coleman.

As Reverend Coleman walked in, he said, "Hey, Dan, I am glad to see you. How is Alma doing?"

"Hey, Reverend Coleman, Momma is still in the hospital. Daddy told me that she had an operation, and that they were keeping her in the hospital until she is well enough to come home. I thought that Lois was here, but I guess she is at the hospital with Pete," said Dan.

"Yes, Lois and Pete caught a cab this morning and went to the hospital. I ain't seen them since then. Well, you are welcome to stay here as long as you like, even spend the night if you want. I'm going to cook something as soon as I get some rest. Terry, how you and Chuck doing?"

"Sir, we are doing all right. Ms. Sweet gave us a hotdog and some lemonade, then Dan came over here, so we are all right. He always looks out for us," I said.

Reverend Coleman said, "Well, Dan, I am glad you came over, and like I said, you are welcome to stay if you like. It's getting late, so you might as well just stay here. I have some pajamas you can wear if you can get in them. They might be too little for you." He went off to his room and came back with some blue pajamas and handed the m to Dan. "You can go in the bathroom and put them on."

Dan went into the bathroom, came out later with them on. They were tight, and Chuck and I started laughing, so did Reverend Coleman. Dan was big for his age and muscular too. After a while, Reverend Coleman went into the kitchen, and we could hear him putting wood into the stove to fix something to eat for us.

While eating black-eyed peas, fatback, and cornbread at the kitchen table, Dan said, "Reverend Coleman, why do people who believe in God get sick and die and things happen to make them unhappy, even when they pray to God in the name of Jesus Christ? My momma love the Lord, and she prays all the time. It's like God is mad with our family. Momma sick and hurting all the time. Daddy acts like he doesn't love us no more. I don't know where he went with that other woman. If something happens to Momma, I don't know what me and Gloria will do, but I will take care of her and make sure that she is all right. I don't care what I have to do. Will you pray for us, pray for my family, especially Momma? I don't know who wrote the Bible, but my momma reads it and believes that she is reading God's word, and she trusts in God's word. You are a preacher, and you read the Bible. Do you believe the Bible is God's word too?"

Rev. Coleman put his hand on Dan's shoulder and said, "Son, I don't have all the answers, but I know God does. Terry, go in my room and get my Bible and bring it to me."

When I brought the Bible in and handed it to him, he took it and started going through the pages. Then he said, "Dan, we are going to pray for your family, especially your mother. However, I want to read something to you out of the Bible. You see, the Bible was written by men who were inspired by God. When Christians, or some who call themselves believers in God, refer to the Bible as being inspired by God, they are to the belief that it contains the word of God. The word 'inspired' can be translated as 'God breathed,' and so unlike other books which have been written by humans, the Bible is special and unique as its God's word. Some books were written to inform, while others were written to reform, but only the Bible was written to transform. Let's look in the book of Second Timothy, the third chapter and the sixteenth and seventeenth verses, and it reads, 'All scripture is given by inspiration of God, and is profitable for doctrine, for reproof, and for correction, for instruction in righteousness. That the man of God may be perfect, thoroughly furnished unto all good works.' So as believer in God, when we want to speak to God, we pray. And when we want to hear from him, we search the scriptures, for his words are spoken through his prophets. He will then teach us as we listen to the promptings of the Holy Spirit. And if God were to call your momma home to be with him in heaven, that will be a blessing for her, and she is a true believer in God, and she will surely be in heaven with God someday. The Bible tells us in Ecclesiastes, chapter 3, verses 1 through 15, 'There is a time for everything, and a season for every activity under the Heavens. A time to be born and a time to die, a time to plant and a time to uproot, a time to kill and a time to heal, a time to tear down and a time to build, a time to weep and a time to laugh, a time to mourn and a time to dance. A time to scatter stones and a time gather them, a time to embrace and a time to refrain from embracing, a time to search and a time to give up, a time to keep and a time to throw away, a time to tear and a time to mend, a time to be silent and a time to speak, a time to love and a time to hate, a time for war and a time for peace.'

"Dan, I believe in my heart that God is real, and he will let you know that he is real. But that does not mean we won't have heartache, pain, and the loss of loved ones. In the book of Hebrews, chapter 9, verse 27, it tells us that it is appointed to everyone to die. And I believe that when we do leave this earth and give up our human body, our spirit will rise during the rapture, and we will go to be with the Lord in heaven. In the book of John, Jesus, the Son of God, said in the fourteenth chapter, verses 1, 2, and 3, 'Let not your heart be troubled; you believe in God, believe also in Me. In My Father's house are many mansions; if it were not so, I would have told you. I go to prepare a place for you, I will come again and receive you to Myself; that where I am, there you may be also.' One thing for sure, God is real in my life and in my heart. I am at peace, and when the Lord calls me home, I imagine I will have a smile on my face. I will be ready. Won't be no crying in heaven, no more pain and suffering. There's this song called, 'Walk Around Heaven All Day' by The Caravans, with Cassietta George singing the lead. Let me tell you, Dan, when I hear that song, it makes me want to go right on to heaven, but since it ain't my time yet,"—Rev. Coleman started singing, surprising us, with a smooth voice—"*I just wait for one of these mornings, it won't be very long, you will look for me, and I'll be gone, I'm going to a place where I won't have nothing to do. I'll just walk around all day. My mother will be waiting and my father too.*"

"You sound good. I didn't know that you can sing like that Rev. Coleman," I said.

"Well, when you get my age, you can do just about anything, son. Dan, if you will, I would like to pray with you. Come on, Terry and Chuck, let's all hold hands and bow your heads. 'Dear heavenly Father, in the name of Jesus Christ, we come to you in prayer, thanking you for your many blessings and asking for your continuous mercy. Lord, we come to you praying that your will, will be done. And we come with a heavy heart, especially Dan. We pray for Alma, and that she recovers from her surgery, but if it is your will to take her to heaven, then we pray for the strength, oh Lord, that you will comfort her children, grandchildren, and all those dear to her, oh Lord.' Now I want y'all to repeat after me. 'Dear Lord Jesus, I know that I am a sinner and ask your forgiveness. I believe you died for my sins and rose from the dead. I turn from my sins and invite you to come into my heart and life. I want to trust and follow you as my Lord and Savior.' Now this prayer alone does not save you. If you want to receive the salvation that is available through Jesus, place your faith in him. Fully trust in his death as the sufficient sacrifice for your sins. Completely rely on him alone as your savior. By all means, say a prayer to God. Tell God how thankful you are for Jesus. Offer praise to God for his love and sacrifice. Thank Jesus for dying for your sins and providing salvation for you. And know and believe that Jesus rose on the third day, seen by many, before ascending to heaven to be with the Father God, leaving the Holy Spirit to be with us. That is the biblical connection between salvation and prayer. God knows your heart. He even knows how many hairs you have on your head. God is omniscient. He knows everything. He knows what you want to pray about before you start to pray, which is why in the book of Matthew, the sixth chapter, and verses 9 through 13, it states, 'Our Father, who art in heaven, hallowed be thy name; thy kingdom come; thy will be done on earth as it is in heaven. Give us this day, our daily bread; and forgive us our trespasses as we forgive those who trespass against us; and lead us not into temptation but deliver us from evil. Amen.' Now you all need to go to bed and get some sleep. If Lois come home while you are asleep, I will wake you, if she lets me. Good night, and may God bless you, Dan. You too, Terry and Chuck."

"Good night, Reverend Coleman," we all chimed in.

Waking up on July 17, 1965, was a quiet sunny morning. Reverend Coleman was singing that same song from last night. (*One of these mornings, it won't be very long, you will look for me, I'll will be gone, I'm going to a place, where I'll have nothing, nothing, nothing to do, but I'll just walk around, walk around heaven all day. When I get to heaven, I'm gonna jump and shout. Nobody will be able to put me out. My mother will be waiting, and my father too. So we'll just join together and just walk around, walk around heaven all day.*)

As I heard the footsteps coming up the stairs, I knew it was Lois's, and I looked over at Dan on the other bunk bed; he was already sitting up and started to cry as we could hear Lois crying as she ascended the steps slowly. We heard Reverend Coleman say, "Oh my god, come here. I am so sorry, God, no!"

Dan fell back on the bunk bed, put the pillow over his head, and was heaving and crying like a baby. Chuck started to cry and went to the stairway where Lois was, and I followed him. Reverend Coleman was sitting on the steps with Lois, both were crying, and I cried because I knew Momma was never coming home again. Lois was screaming so loud. Then she started talking and crying at the same time, unlike ever before.

"Coleman, why God take my momma? She was all right, and now she is gone! Lord, have mercy. Why, God? Why did you take my momma, knowing we need her? Why, Lord, why? Oh my god! Where's Chuck and Terry at?" Lois said while sobbing.

"They are at the top of the stairs, looking down here at us. They heard you, and Dan is up there too. He spent the night here last night," said Reverend Coleman.

Lois jumped up and ran up the steps and went into the room where Dan was laying on the bed. Lois had him to sit up, hugging him and crying with him, tried to console him, saying, "Dan, it's going to be all right. Momma is in a better place now. You can stay with me, Gloria can too, so don't you worry. I know it hurts right now. We are going to hurt because we love her so much. Momma will always live on in our hearts and in our minds. She will always be with us no matter where we are. It's okay to cry, but she is in a better place now. No more pain and suffering. She is gone to be with the Lord now. She is in heaven, looking down on us. You still got me and Pete and Gloria too, and Coleman is here for you, and Bill too." Lois started humming, the same way Momma did, while she reached for me and Chuck. As we walked over to her, she hugged all three of us, swaying back and forward. Then Reverend Coleman came over and hugged us all while quietly praying as Lois continued to hum.

After a while, Lois, knowing she had to be strong for everyone, being she was the oldest, wishing Pete was here since she was the most mature, said, "Dan, get dressed, and let me take a bath and get dressed. We need to walk on The Block and get a cab so we can go get Gloria and see Pete and let Aunt Leatha know about Momma. I don't know where Bud and Luther are, probably in Durham."

After Lois and Dan got dressed and was about to leave, giving me and Chuck a hug, telling us to be good and giving us a kiss, and Reverend Coleman a kiss too. Reverend Coleman said, "Lois, here, take this money. It's a couple hundred dollars, and do with it what you need to do. I will go to the bank and get some more before the bank closes. Dan and Gloria are going to need some new clothes and shoes, so don't you worry about nothing. I will pay Sweet to look out for Terry and Chuck unless you want to take them with you. I will be leaving in a little while."

Lois said, "I will speak with Sweet and Betty on my way down. She will let Pumpkin come up here and make them some breakfast and get them dressed and keep them until I get back. I will give her a few dollars, so don't worry. Coleman, thanks so very much. You are a kind man and a good husband. Keep us in your prayers. I love you."

We watched as Lois and Dan went down the stairs, and we went to the window and watched them until they turned onto James Street. As Reverend Coleman was about to leave, Pumpkin knocked on the door, and Reverend Coleman opened the door and let her inside as he was leaving.

CHAPTER 10

Moving to Brooklyn, New York

After the funeral, everyone gathered over to Aunt Porter's house. All the children had to go outside. Dan and Gloria were inside with all the other adults. Gloria was always by Daddy's side. I was outside with Tony, Chuck, and Greg—sitting on the front porch. We could hear them inside. Lois was yelling at Daddy, and Pete was yelling at him too, also at that woman who came with Daddy all the way from New York. Although we couldn't hear what was being said, we all knew that Lois and Pete were mad at Daddy because of that woman named Jewel. It was being said by everybody that she took Daddy away from Momma, breaking her heart and breaking up our home.

Dan came outside and sat on the porch with us, and I asked, "Dan, why Lois and Pete in the fussing?"

Dan just started shaking his head and said, "They are mad because Daddy wants to take me and Gloria back with him and Jewel to Brooklyn, New York. But I told him I'm not going back with him, that I was going to stay right here. But Gloria wants to go with him, and I think Lois and Pete are going to let her go. But I am staying here, so don't worry. They don't like that woman. Daddy had known her for a long time too. She is from Fair Bluff, just like Daddy. But she told Pete that she has been living in Brooklyn for a long time. I thought Lois was going to hit her, but Daddy got in the way, and Pete started to get her too. You know how they are. If one gets at you, so will the other one."

Just then Pete came outside, and said, "I know that y'all are hurting and missing Momma already, but it's going to be all right. Dan, you can stay with me, and you can stay with Lois too. You don't have to go to New York, so don't you worry about that. Daddy wants you to stay with Aunt Leatha, but you are going to stay with one of us. Momma is in heaven, with God now. She doesn't hurt anymore, and she is looking down on us right now. She is in a better place. No more suffering or pain. Gloria is going to move to New York with Daddy, but she will come to visit every summer and spend two months with us. So you will see her again, and the summer will be back again so fast that y'all won't even get a chance to miss her. It will be like she never left, and she will be out here in a minute to say goodbyes to all of you. Aunt Leatha told me and Lois to make sure y'all eat, so I want y'all to come on in the kitchen so I can fix y'all a plate of food. Everyone, go wash your hands and face. Dan, get them a washcloth and help Greg and Chuck, then bring them into the kitchen." Pete walked off to the kitchen to prepare plates for to eat.

People was coming and going to give their condolences, making sure they stop to speak with Dan. Everyone knew that he adored his mother, especially with him being the only boy in the family. As we all sat in the kitchen, eating fried chicken, potato salad, and collards, Ms. Viola came into the kitchen, dressed in her elegant black skirt suit, with her tiny little black shoe, and started telling Pete that she was sorry for her loss, and that she came to give the family her condolences.

She then turned to Dan, hugging him, then said, "Hey, baby Dan, I am so very sorry for y'all loss. I know how devastated you all must be. But just know that your momma is in heaven now. Yeah, the Lord called her home to be with him. You know that the Bible tells us that in John 14:1–3, 'Let not your heart be troubled; you believe in God, believe also in Me. In my Father's house are many mansions; if it were not so, I would have told you. I go to prepare a place for you. And if I go and prepare a place for you, I will come again and receive you to Myself; that where I am, there you may be also.' You see, Alma loved the Lord and spent most her day praying for you and all her children and giving thanks to the Lord for everything. And I know that she is in heaven right now, looking down on us. The Bible goes on to say, 'I also pray that you will understand the incredible greatness of god's power for us who believe in him. This is the same mighty power that raised Christ form the dead and seated him in the place of honor at God's right hand in the Heavenly realms.' That's what the Bible says in the book of Ephesians 1:19–20. Did you know that the apostle Paul, who briefly visited paradise during a special revelation, was so eager to get back there? He thought about dying so he could go be with God because it was so much better than being here on earth, saying that he would rather 'be present with the Lord.' That's somewhere in the book of the Second Corinthians. All I'm trying to say is that Alma is in heaven and doing just fine, and you can best believe that she is still praying for all y'all and probably talking to God about all of y'all right now. I know that some people don't believe in God or heaven and hell. But I know Alma definitely believed in the Lord Jesus Christ, and I am here to tell you that anything that the mind can conceive and believe, it surely will achieve. And you best believe that Alma is in heaven. Well, I must go now. I will be going to up to heaven one day." Ms. Viola started singing as she walked out of the kitchen. *"I know I'm going upper yonder, I'm going upper yonder, to be with my Lord."*

As we finished eating, Pete said we can go back outside. So we all went outside on the front porch. Lois came outside and said, "Dan, you are going to stay here with Aunt Bent. Pete is going to stay here with you too. But you can come and see me anytime you want too, and you can stay with me and Coleman too. We are going to be leaving in a few minutes. I called a cab. Let me know when he pulls up. I am going to go back in here to say goodbye to everybody else. Gloria is going back with Daddy, so I am going to let her know that me and Pete will come up there and get her and bring her back home if we have too. I already gave her my address, so she can write me. Dan, you know where we live, and you know that Terry and Chuck want to see you as much as possible. Pete said she is not going back to the house because she is scared and refuses to stay there since Momma is gone to heaven. I will be back out in a minute, but don't forget to come and get me when the cab gets here, Dan. Terry, don't let Chuck and Greg get off the porch."

Dan said, "I will let you know when the cab gets here, and I'm watching them, so they will be all right. Terry, look, here comes Pa Wright with his horse and buggy. He is stopping too. I guess he's coming to express his condolences."

"Hey, Dan, here comes Mr. Jesse and Mr. Raymond walking together, and I can see the cab coming too," I said.

Mr. Jesse and Mr. Raymond came up to Dan, and both hugged him and was talking to him. Dan started walking toward us and went into the house with them.

Tony said, "Terry, I remember Mr. Raymond. I went to his store with you and Dan, and we got some cookies and a coke and BC powder for Momma. We can't go there no more and get Momma some more BC powder and a coke because she went to heaven."

Terry looked at Tony and put his hand around his shoulder and said, "We can still go there, but Momma don't need no more BC powder and cokes, because like Ms. Viola said a while ago in the kitchen, Momma don't hurt no more. She is in a better place now."

When Pa Wright walked up to the porch, before he could say anything, Chuck asked him, "Pa Wright, can I go and see your horse, and can I ride on you wagon too?"

Pa Wright said, "Well, son, you will have to ask Lois, but right now is not the time, I believe." Then he walked on into the house.

"Chuck we are getting ready to go anyway, but when we come to see Aunt Bent, and if we see him, he will let us ride on his wagon. He doesn't care," I said.

Lois put out with her arm around Dan and was saying, "Don't worry because if you change your mind, once Daddy leave and you want to come stay with me, I will come and get you and help you get your things. You will be all right. Pete will be here with you, and I will be checking on you too. Come on, Terry and Chuck, let's go. Bye, Tony and Greg, we will be back to see y'all soon."

We went to the cab, and Lois got in the front, and we got in the back. As we pulled off, I saw Daddy came outside and was looking at us as drove off. Standing there in a blue pin-striped suit and a blue hat on his head, with his jet-black hair shining, such a handsome man.

Lois was talking to the man that was driving, and people were walking by, going to Aunt Bent's house. People would wave at us and say something to Lois since we were moving very slowly. Once we turned onto Canal Street, Lois was saying, "I told Pete that Momma came to me in my dreams and was asking me 'What have they done to me?' and it was so real. She told me not to worry, and that she was going to be all right, and to tell Pete too because she would tell her, but she knows Pete would be scared. Coleman said I woke up scream-ing and sweating. But I don't remember being scared or nothing like that, and even though I knew in the dream that I was dreaming, it was still so real. I am telling you the truth. Lord, this world won't never be the same without Momma. And poor Dan, he's so quiet all the time, and I know he is hurting more than all of us. I will never understand how Dr. Miller can remove a tumor out of her stomach, and then she dies a week later. The doctor said that the tumor was malignant though, so I guess she had cancer. Momma didn't smoke or chew tobacco, or dip snuff, so I just don't understand. She prob-ably would have been better off if Dr. Hayes was her doctor. But he is from Washington, DC, and I know those White Doctors don't even want to acknowledge him as a doctor. He's probably a much better doctor than they are, and I know that he really cares about his patients. Gloria will be all right as long as she is with Daddy. He loves her, if he doesn't love nobody else. You got to look over me. I had a few drinks, and I'm just talking and talking."

The cab driver said, "It's all right, Lois. I know that you and your family are devasted with the passing of your Momma. I want you to know that I am sincerely sorry for your loss. You are right though, the world won't ever be the same again. But as they say, she will live on in our hearts and minds. I lost my mother a few years ago, so I know what you and your family are going through right now. It hurts now, and it's going to always hurt, but it will get easier, and life will go on. You just have to remember all the good times and all the conversations you had, especially the good ones, and the lessons she taught you."

As we reached home, Lois reached into her purse, asking," How much do I owe you for bringing us home?"

The cab driver said, "You don't owe me anything. Reverend Coleman was at the cab stand when you called, and he paid me for you. He wanted to ride with me, but we didn't know how many were coming back with you. He said to tell you not to worry about cooking, that he was going by Holloway's Bar-B-Que on his way home. I am going to pick him up and I will bring him back, but first, I must run out to the hospital and pick up someone and take them to Pikeville."

"Well, okay, thank you. Tell Coleman I said thanks, and that I love him. Terry, you and Chuck come on. Let's get into the house. I want y'all to change your clothes, so you can come back outside and play."

Sweet was on her porch and said, "Hey, Lois, I know I said a lot already, but still, I am so sorry for your loss. Anytime you want to talk, just let me know. I will come up there, or you can come down here. I made some sweet potato pies just for you and the kids. I will send them up by Stuff. You know he wants to see Terry."

"Oh, thank you so much, Sweet. You are so sweet. That's why everybody calls you 'Sweet'," said Lois.

After we changed clothes, Lois called us into the kitchen, where she was making some grape Kool-Aid and told us to sit down for a moment so she could talk to us. She said, "I know you both are hurting right now. I am too. But everything is going to be just fine, so I don't want you to worry. And both of y'all have been calling Momma all your lives. Alma Floyd Bullock is my momma and Pete's momma and Dan's momma and Gloria's momma. Terry, she was your grand-momma. I am your momma, and I am Chuck's momma too. Pete and Gloria are your aunts because they are my sisters. Dan is your uncle because he is my brother. Uncle Bud and Uncle Luke are your grand- or great-uncles because they are momma's brothers. Leatha and Momma are sisters, and they are your grand- or great-aunts. But

Terry, you practically grew up with Dan and Gloria, so they are like a brother and sister to you and Tony. And they will always be like a sister and brother to you, so will Tony and Gregory too. I know that for a long time you use to think that I was your sister. So I want you to know that I have always taken care of you both, and I will always take very good care of you and Chuck. So I don't want either of you to worry about nothing. Now since Momma is gone, I am the only Momma you got now, and Terry, you stop calling me girl and call me Momma from now on. Momma will always be with us. She is with us now because we are talking about her. She will be with us when we think about her and when we remember how she look and what she sounds like and some of the things she said to us. That's why people say when someone goes to heaven, they live on in our hearts and minds. Our family won't ever be the same again with Momma gone up to heaven. And then Daddy is going to divide our family even more tomorrow when he takes Gloria back up to New York with him and that hussy Jewel. I can't stand that hussy. That woman just came into our lives and tore our family apart, and Daddy is just as guilty as she is. But we are Bullocks, we are strong, and we are all going to be all right. And I promise that I will keep us together. Coleman is a good man, and he is your stepdaddy now, Terry, so I want you to be respectful and mind him. You will still get to see Desi, so don't you worry. Now go on outside and play. Take Chuck with you and look out for him, just like Dan looked out for you. He is your baby brother, and he loves you and looks up to you the way you look up to Dan. Tell Sweet I will be down there as soon as I finish cleaning up, or she can come up here."

"Momma, I will tell her, and I will look out for Chuck too," I said.

Lois looked up in surprise and said, "Aaw, come and give me hug, Terry. That's the first time you called me Momma."

The next spring, Pete and Dan came to see Momma. Momma and Pete was in the kitchen. Dan came into the bedroom where we were. We could hear them talking, and Pete was telling her that Dan stayed at home, and that she wasn't going to stay in that house because she was afraid she might see grandmomma.

Lois was telling her, "Pete, when I saw Momma, she told me that she came to me because she didn't want to scare you because she knew that you are scared of dead people. But I don't believe we will see her anymore, not until we get to heaven anyway."

Pete said, "Well, I'm going to stay with Bent until I get myself together. I'm not going back into that house, not at nighttime anyway. Anyway, girl, give us something to drink. We walked all the way up here. Dan, come and get you some lemonade. Hey, Chuck and Terry."

Dan went into the kitchen, and we both spoke to Aunt Pete, and she gave us a hug before going back in the kitchen with Momma. Dan came back in the room with us, being quiet as he usually was. We all were still hurt and sad because of Momma.

Chuck said, "Dan, what's wrong with you? Why are you sad?"

Dan looked at Chuck and said, "Chuckie, that is a good question, and I see you are going to be smart, just like Terry. Well, I can give you a lot of reasons why I am sad, especially now that Momma is gone to heaven. But I am thinking about going to Brooklyn so I can check on Gloria and look out for her. She has been gone a long time, and we never got a letter from her or Daddy. I've been thinking about going there for a long time. When I do go there, I will still come back home so we can be together."

We all were listening to Aunt Pete and Momma talk. Pete said, "On the way up here, Dan was telling me that he was ready to go to New York because he wants to make sure that Gloria will be all right up there in a strange place. And that we are grown-ups, and he knows that we will be all right. He wasn't asking me. He was letting me know."

Momma said, "Dan, come in here for a minute."

When Dan got in the kitchen, Pete said, "Dan, tell Lois what you told me on the way up here, about wanting to go to New York."

Before he could speak, Lois said, "Dan, if you go to New York, I want you to promise us that you will come back home to visit us and bring Gloria with you. And when you get there and don't like it, come back home. We will come up there and get you if we have too. And you are going to need to take your birth certificate with you, so we will have to go to the courthouse to the clerk of court and get it. Coleman has a suitcase. I can give you. And we'll get you a ticket and give you some spending money too. So when you are ready to go, just let me know, okay?"

Dan just said, "Lois, I'm ready to go now so I can see Gloria. I know she misses me."

"Well, I have to work tomorrow, but I go in at noon. Come over here in the morning, and we will go and get your birth certificate before I go to work. I will stop by and get your ticket and see what time the bus leaves. You can stay with me tonight, and that way you can spend some time with Terry and Chuckie before you leave, okay?" said Lois.

Dan came in the room with me and Chuck, and we could hear Pete still talking to Reverend Coleman, and then Pete said, "I heard what you talking to Dan. What was you telling him?"

Lois said, "Nothing, just letting him know that he can always come back home to us, and that we would come up there and get him if we have too, or send him money to get back home. And he will need his birth certificate and social security card to take with him. And he is going to stay over here so I can take him to get it in the morning before I go to work."

Pete said, "Well, I am getting ready to go. It's getting late. I will get a cab, if I can't get Willie to take me home. I will see you later, Coleman, and Dan, I love you. You are going to be all right. Bye, Terry and Chuckie. You too, Lois."

We stayed up talking until it was late. Dan was playing with Chuckie, tossing him up in the air and catching him when he came down, something he used to do with Chuckie and Tony. Greg and Rocky were too young for him to toss them; they were still toddlers, too young, and would cry when he tried to do it to them, but Dan said it would make them tougher. But Chuckie seemed to enjoy it, just as I used too when I was smaller.

"Dan, when are you going to come back when you leave tomorrow?" I asked.

Dan said, "I don't know yet, but I'm coming back. I won't ever forget you and all the rest of the family. We are family no matter where we are. That won't ever change. We have the same blood, and that's what makes us family."

Reverend Coleman and Lois came into the room and said it was time to go to sleep, and it was time for us to say our prayers. We all got on our knees and bowed our heads, and Reverend Coleman said, "Our Father, who art in heaven. Hallowed be thy name. Thy kingdom come, thy will be done in earth as it is in heaven. Give us this day, our daily bread. And forgive us our trespasses as we forgive those who trespass against us. And lead us not into temptation but deliver us from evil. For thine is the kingdom and the power and the glory, forever, amen."

Then Lois said, "Okay, now go to sleep. Dan, we are going to leave early so we can be at the clerk's office when they open in the morning at nine. Good night. Chuckie and Terry, go to sleep."

After they turned the lights out, and left the room, Dan said, "Terry, I might be back for Christmas, right after my birthday. Sleep on that, and goodnight. You too, Chuckie."

The next morning, we could hear Lois in the bathroom singing; she always liked to sing in the mornings when she was in the bathroom. When she came out, she said, "Dan, go on in the bathroom. I put a toothbrush and washcloth on the sink, and put those pajamas in your suitcase. Coleman said you can take them with you. He is gone. He had to go with Reverend Pate to work on the church but told me to tell you that he is going to keep you in prayer and to take care of yourself. Oh, he also told me to tell you not to be a stranger, that you are always welcome in our home. I am going to get dressed and then make some breakfast, your favorite: eggs, grits, and bacon. And I am going to fix you some sandwiches to take with you and sixty dollars Coleman gave me to give to you. Terry, when Dan finishes, go in there and wash up. Don't forget to brush your teeth, and Dan, help Chuckie. Terry, you and Chuckie are going to stay with Sweet until Coleman comes home. I want you to be good, and don't you and Stuff be going around on that block either, not even over to Doris's house. Stay in the yard and play where Sweet can keep an eye on y'all, all right?"

"She's not going to let us go nowhere anyway," I said.

After we ate breakfast, Lois said, "It's cold outside, so get your heavy coats and toboggans and put them on. Dan, help Chuckie put his coat and hat on so we can go. I don't know how long it's going to take, so we need to get on down there so we can be there when they open up."

Lois went down the stairs to go see Sweet and ask her to keep us. After helping Chuckie with his coat and hat, Dan picked him up, and we went down the stairs. Sweet was in her doorway, and Lois was coming off the porch. She stopped and gave me and Chuckie a hug and told us to be good. We watched as they left walking down Center Street toward downtown, where the court was. Dan was almost as tall as Lois; she was five-eleven, or six feet tall. We watched until they were out of sight, and we couldn't see them anymore. Chuckie was crying because Lois was leaving as he always did. Me, I was crying because Dan was leaving me for the first time in my life, and I didn't know when I was going to see him again. The sky was dark, and it was coldest day of my life.

CHAPTER 11

Letters from Paris Island: Marines

Later that night, we could hear Lois coming up the stairs. As we ran to the top of the stairs, Reverend Coleman was already there to meet her. He was always looking out of the window, so I knew that he had seen her coming. Chuckie and I usually be outside to greet her; we could see her in her white dress as soon as she turned onto Elm Street. We knew what time she came home from work and was always happy to see her. But on this evening, a thunderstorm was wreaking havoc over Goldsboro, North Carolina.

As Lois got to the top of the stairs, she said, "Oh my goodness, it is pouring down, raining out there. I forgot to take an umbrella with me. I had to go to work after I took Dan to the clerk of court to get his birth certificate. He needs to have his birth certificate. It can help him get a job in Brooklyn, and he will be able to take care of himself and Gloria too and be able to come back home when he wants too. Dan thinks he can use his birth certificate to go into the army or the marines when he gets to New York, but I don't know how since his birth certificate says he was born in 1953. Then we walked to the bus station and got his ticket to Brooklyn, New York. I told him to call me when he got there, and he has enough money to come right back if he doesn't like it there."

Reverend Coleman said, "Well, he knows he has a home here when he gets ready to come back home. He will need a job. I don't think they will let him in the military because he would have to take written tests and a physical. He may be able to pass a physical, but not the tests. I really don't know Lois, and with the Vietnam War going on as it is, he doesn't need to be going into the military, at least not until he is eighteen years old. Shucks, grown men are moving to Canada and Mexico to evade going into the military, not to mention the rich one's going into college, so they won't have to go in the military. Dan is young, and he's still in a lot of pain and hurting from Alma's passing. His whole world has been turned upside down. But what's done has been done, and all we can do now is pray for him."

Lois said, "Dan will be all right. He can take care of himself. Daddy will be glad to have him up there with him. I know that Gloria will be glad to see him. I guess it's only right that he is going up there. It's not like he is grown yet. But I do wish he would stay here with us. I'm going to really miss him. Sometimes I feel that our family is cursed. You know, they say that my grandmomma, Pinky Floyd, could put spells on people and make people have bad luck. So maybe it all have backfired because everything seems to be going bad for our family. It's like a black cloud has been hanging over our family, and even Goldsboro. It might be good that Dan is getting away from here and going to New York. Coleman, do you believe in bad luck?"

Coleman said, "Well, I believe that if you accept Jesus Christ in your life and stay on the path that God wants you to be on, that everything will go according to his plan. That's what I believe, Lois, and I have prayed with Dan. He accepted the Lord Jesus in his life, and maybe it's God's will that he goes to New York. But as far as bad luck goes, I believe that you make your own luck. And if all went by the golden rule by doing unto others as we will have them do unto us, then this world would be a better place to live in for everybody. Like I mentioned before, Dan is hurting from the loss of his mother. You all are. But some people hurt more than others, especially those that love the most. Some people grieve more than others and longer than most other people. I believe it will be good for him to be around his daddy and little sister. He has a lot of love in him, and I believe he will become to love the Lord in due time. The seed has already been planted by his mother. He has a good heart, and it's broken right now. His heart will heal being with his daddy, and especially with his baby sister. I have talked with him a lot, and I can tell he is not only adventurous, but very caring and loving."

"Terry, I see you out there. You can come in here. We are just talking about Dan," said Lois.

I said, "Chuck is already asleep, and I am getting ready to go to sleep too. I was just gonna tell y'all good night. Do you think Dan is in New York yet? How far away is it?"

Lois said, "Well, by the time you wake up, he will be there. He will have change buses, but he will get there later tonight. I asked the man at the bus station how far it was, and he told us that it was about seven hundred miles away. He was telling Dan how big the city was and how the people talked different, with a different proper accent. And he told him that people up there was not as friendly as they are down here, and that they don't speak when you speak to them unless they really know you. So Dan knows a little of what to expect when he gets up there. He will be just fine, so don't you worry about him. Dan will be back to visit with us soon. Maybe for his birthday and Christmas. Anyway, give me a kiss, and you go into bed now. I love you."

Terry walked to the bed, gave her a kiss, and said, "Good night, Momma, and Reverend Coleman."

Rev. Coleman said, "Goodnight, son. Don't forget to say your prayers."

"Yes, sir," Terry replied.

We lived on the corner of Elm Street and Center Street, right in front of the Dave Bryant Five Playboy Club. We lived upstairs, and Sweet and her family lived downstairs. When Dan left, I started to hang out with some other guys in the neighborhood—some who knew Dan, like the two brothers, John and Lee-Lee, who were the same age as Dan, and there was Donald Brooks, he was left-handed, who was my age at the time, yet I learned how to box southpaw from him. There were also two brothers, Jerry and Willie. John taught us all how to box and was surprised at how much Dan had taught me and how much I knew about boxing and how good I was. We all would stand around and sing songs. We would help Joe Tex and Millie Jackson and other singers set up their band equipment in the Playboy Club on the weekends to make a few dollars. We even got to stay and see them perform until it got late. We all had to go home before it got too late. On the weekdays, we would go around to the Budweiser warehouse and unload the yeast off the truck to make money. Every day, we would all get together—sing, score on each other, tell jokes, and box.

One day, John told us that they were having a boxing contest at the E. A. House Boy's Club, and they were going by age, and that we all should enter the contest. We all agreed, except Jerry and Willie. So we started to practice more; everyone seemed surprised that I could always get the best of Donald. I would rely on all that I learned from Dan and Big Dave, especially flicking my left hand out and then throwing an overhand right, flicking it right at the point of impact on the opponent's chin, delivering a devasting blow that usually lead to a knockout blow.

On the day of the boxing event, I was paired up with my cousin, Look Up. I didn't want to box him, but he was eager to box me. I knocked him out in a just a few seconds, and everyone was cheering. John and Lee-Lee picked me up and was bragging about me. I remember wishing Dan could be there because I knew he would be proud of me. Dan always told me that I would always surprise people. Because of my looks, they couldn't see my intelligence, determination, and heart. I remember my cousin Jack beat Donald, and I had to fight him next. We watched as John beat Chester, but no one was surprised. Lee-Lee chose not to fight, and John was still trying to convince him when it was time for me to fight Jack. Jack was a few years older than me and very confident. He kept saying what he was going to do to me before he knocks me out. When Dave said "Go," Jack came at me very fast, so I didn't have time to flick my left. I just threw an overhand right as fast and hard as I could. Jack rushed into my overhand right, and I hit him in the nose, knocking him down. Then Dave stopped the fight because Jack's nose was bleeding. I won my age category and received a plaque and twenty-five dollars. Jack was really mad at me and threatened to get me when I came over to his house; his mother, Doris, is my first cousin. I told him that I had to come over there, and that Dave won't be there to stop me the next time. We never fought again, but I always stayed alert when I was around him.

When I got home, I told Momma that I won a trophy in boxing and twenty-five dollars. I thought she was going to be upset at me, but she hugged me and said she was proud of me. We sat down in the kitchen, and she said, "I can't wait to tell Dan. I know that he will be very proud of you, Terry. Now tell me what happened."

"I just did what Big Dave and Dan taught me how to do, and I had to box Look-Up. He didn't even hit me. I just knocked him out. Then I had to box Jack, and he didn't hit me either. I hit him in the nose, and Dave stopped the fight. He told us that if anyone got hurt or started to bleed, that he would stop the fight, so I made him stop the fight. Then Jack said he was going to get me when he catches me over his house. I told him the next time I won't stop. I'm not scared of him. He just run his mouth. He can't fight me."

Lois said, "I am going to tell Desi and Doris he better not bother you. If he does, the next time, knock him down and kick right in the head. If you beat him bad enough, he won't bother you no more. Don't let nobody hit you in your face or try to scare you by talking junk."

Terry looked at Lois and said, "He doesn't scare me. I already told him I won't stop the next time. He can't beat me."

"Terry, we are going to move soon. Coleman found a house on the corner of Canal Street and Holt Street. You will still be going to School Street School and can still go to the Boy's Club. Lord knows that I am tired of walking up and down these steps. We will still be in Little Washington. Aunt Agnus and Aunt Bent lives on Canal Street, just two blocks away across from Mr. Jesse's store, and Clara is on Orchard Street. Y'all use to go there all the time, you and Dan. You know where it is. You just didn't go down that way. It's a block off Pine Street. We should be moving the first of the month, so we will be in our new home by Thanksgiving. So when Dan comes back home, he will have his own bedroom," said Lois.

I asked, "Well, when is Dan coming back home?"

Lois said, "I don't know yet, but I expect he will be home some time in December. Hopefully for his birthday, or Christmas. If not, then some time next year. You are going to be just fine. We all are. I want you to be a good big brother to Chuckie, just like Dan is to you, and always will be to you. He looks up to you just like you look up to Dan. Chuckie, come in here. Terry, do y'all want some lemonade and some of this peach pie?" Chuckie walked into the kitchen and leaned on Terry.

Terry helped Chuckie get into his chair as Lois placed a piece of pie in a saucer in front of him and Terry. Then she gave them a glass of lemonade. As we ate, she went to her room, and we could hear the music playing, and she always sang to the music. Stevie Wonder was singing "For Once In My Life."

Lois said, "Terry, this is for you and Chuckie," and started to sing, coming back into the kitchen, and singing to Chuckie and me. "'*For once in my life, I have someone who needs me, someone I've needed so long. For once, unafraid, I can go where life leads me. Somehow I know I'll be strong. For once I can touch what my heart use to dream of long before I knew. Oooh, someone warm like you two would make my dreams come true. Yeah, yeah, yeah, for once in my life, I won't let sorrow hurt me, not like it did with the passing of my momma.*' *Whew*! Let me sit down. I love that song. I can't help but think of Momma, and with Gloria and Dan being in New York. But I thank the Lord that I got you and Chuckie. I know y'all won't desert me. Give me a hug. I love you both so very much." Lois started to put away the saucers and glasses as we went in the living room. I could still hear her humming that song, something that Momma used to do all the time.

We finally moved to Canal Street in the summer of 1968, in a big white house, with three bedrooms. The backyard was big and had a big pecan tree and two fig trees. The front yard also had a pecan tree. The front porch was big, with a rail all the way across. As we were moving in, it seemed that everyone that I went to school with was there to welcome us into the new neighborhood. The Whitakers lived across from us—the Hobbs, Smiths, Kings, Waters, Jacksons, Barnes, and many more, who had children my age. Momma was the happiest that I had seen her in a long time. Ladies started to bring platters of food, cakes, and vegetables. Reverend Coleman just sat on the front porch with a look of contentment on his face. Happy to see Momma interact with the new neighbors, although she seems to know most of them. I was happy to learn that our phone was already working because I didn't want Dan to call, and we'll not get to talk to him. And I wanted to call Tony because Aunt Pete had moved around the corner on Persimmons Street, just three blocks away. We had a woodstove, and Reverend Coleman taught me how to cut wood the proper way so I wouldn't hurt myself. I learned a lot from him and really enjoyed the time that I got to spend with him. He bought me and Chuckie suits, ties, and new shinny shoes and white shirts, like he wore every day, and we would go to church on Sundays. We always sat on the first row. Momma would always wake me up when I fell asleep, but Chuckie would just sleep until we got home. Reverend Coleman bought me my first bicycle, my first football and basketball. But most importantly, he taught me and everyone who came in contact with him the love of God.

We were in the kitchen, eating dinner, when we heard Aunt Pete knocking on the door and yelling for Lois. Momma jumped up from the kitchen table and rushed to the front of the house. We all went to see what the commotion was all about. As I reached the front room, Lois was reading a letter, and Aunt Pete was saying, "Girl, can you believe Dan graduated from boot camp in South Carolina. We are invited to go to his graduation. How in the world is he in the marines. I thought he was in Brooklyn, New York, with Daddy and Gloria Jean."

Lois started crying and said, "I can't believe it either, Pete. He's only fourteen. I just don't see how that happened. According to this letter, he graduated yesterday. Maybe they got the wrong Dan Bullock. Have you tried to call Daddy?"

Pete said, "I tried to call, but I can't get nobody. What do you think we should do?"

Lois kept looking at the letter and finally said, "Well, there's not much we can do, just wait and see if it is really our Dan."

After Pete left, Lois was talking to Reverend Coleman and was saying, "Coleman, I couldn't believe that letter. I tried calling Daddy, and I can't get no answer. I sure hope he don't get into no trouble. Terry, go back outside and play, stop eavesdropping, and take Chuckie with you!

CHAPTER 12

Home after Boot Camp

It seemed that Lois and Pete had decided to keep things quiet about Dan being in the marines and having graduated from basic training. At least until they were sure that it was really "our" Dan. We all could feel that there was something going on, even my little brother Chuckie would ask me when Dan was coming back home. I would ask Reverend Coleman about Dan when Lois wasn't around because we both knew that I went with her to the clerk of court's office. I also knew that she was afraid that she could get into trouble, and even more so afraid now that there was a possibility that Dan was in the marines at the tender age of fourteen. Lois was so afraid that she made me promise not to mention anything about us going to the clerk of court's office. Reverend Coleman was the only other person to know, not even Aunt Pete knew.

It was the month of December, and we all was hoping to see Dan on his birthday and also for Christmas. And if Dan was actually in the marines and graduated, then I was hoping that he would come home. Everyone was waiting for graduation day to get here, hoping that Dan would come home that day or the next day. We only had less than two weeks to wait for his graduation.

The weather was cold and brisk, and I would help Reverend Coleman cut wood. I learned that the harder and faster that I worked, the warmer I would stay. However, I also learned that Reverend Coleman had only one steady speed, slow. This allowed him to work at the same pace for a long time, and no matter what, I could not get him to speed up. When I got tired, he said, "Son, if you pace yourself, you can work longer. It's not about how fast you work. The key is to be safe and do it right. I see you trying to rush. I know it's cold out here, but take your time."

I learned a lot from Reverend Coleman; he taught me things just like Dan did. But still I missed Dan probably more than anyone. I kept wondering if Dan was really in the marines. Dan always said that we were going into the army. Maybe they do have the wrong Dan Bullock, but Lois and Aunt Pete couldn't get in touch with Granddaddy in New York, or that lady Jewel. Dan hasn't called us, so everyone was getting worried now, especially Lois and Aunt Porter.

Pa Wright always came by our house, with his horse and buggy. Lois wouldn't let me ride on the back, even after I told her that me and Dan used to ride with him. So me, Chuckie, Tony, and Greg would just stand on the side of the road and look at that old horse passed by. We always waved at Pa Wright. We would joke that he looked like the horse.

I liked living on Canal Street. It was a dirt road, like most roads in the Black neighborhoods. Not many cars came down Canal Street. Not many Black people had cars; there were only a few.

Mr. Ed had a white Chrysler and a truck. He had a bit saw, and he cut wood and sold it by the cord. Mr. Slick had a store on the corner of Holt Street and Whitfield Street; he also had a blue truck. There were several others, but I didn't know them. Every time I see Mr. Ed and Mr. Slick, they would ask me about Dan and how was he doing. I wondered how they knew, but it seems Granddaddy knew everyone, and everyone seemed to know our family. I learned that everyone in Little Washington were like family to one another. Little Washington was the best section of Goldsboro, North Carolina, located on the West Side. I still never understood why they called it Little Washington, except people would move to Washington DC and, years later, come back to Goldsboro for whatever reason.

Since Momma went to heaven and Gloria and Dan moved to New York, I spent a lot of time by myself. I was always thinking and wondering why things happened to our family. I once heard Lois saying that it was a black cloud over our family. I asked Reverend Coleman what did having a black cloud over our family meant, bad luck? Reverend Coleman reminded me that I didn't have to worry about that as long as I stayed on the right path with Jesus and make good decision in life.

On the sixteenth of December—cold and blustery—the wind was blowing the pecans off the trees in the back and front yards. I asked Lois if I could go outside and pick up the pecans, and she said, "Yeah, you can go there. Just make sure you put on your heavy coat and toboggin." So I got dressed, and Chuckie wanted to go outside too, but she wouldn't let him go with me. I got a bag and went outside; the pecans were everywhere. I thought we had gotten most of them last month. Reverend Coleman told me that the harvest season was between October and December. The pecans were even in the street, and I started getting them up first so Mr. Ed wouldn't rum over them. Just as I began to pick the pecans up, I heard someone yell, "Get back in that yard right now, soldier!" I turned around as quickly as I could and couldn't believe my eyes. It was Dan; he was smiling and walking up to me. I took off running to him and ran right into him, and he picked me up. He had on a uniform, a hat, gloves, and shiny shoes. He was bigger than I remember. He looked older too.

He put me down and said, "Stop crying. You are going to be a marine like me. I know you are glad to see me. I am glad to see you too. Where is Lois and Reverend Coleman?"

I kept looking at him and just couldn't believe he was really here. Finally, I said, "They are in the house. Lois is going to be so happy to see you. Are you going to stay with us?"

Dan said, "I don't know. I might stay with Aunt Bent and Pete and y'all too, but while I am here, I will see you every day so we can spend time together. Terry, you go on in the house first and let them know that I am out here. I don't want to give them a heart attack."

I ran in the house as fast as I could. I went in the living room. Lois and Reverend Coleman were talking. Chuckie was in her lap. I said, "Momma, Dan is here. He is outside and told me to come inside first to tell you he is outside, so y'all won't have a heart attack."

Lois sat there looking at me and said, "Stop playing and telling that lie before I spank your butt."

Just then, there was a loud knock on the door, and Dan said, "Hey, it's getting cold out here. Can I come in?"

Lois jumped up so fast, she almost dumped Chuckie on the floor, and Dan walked into the living. Lois ran up to him and was hugging him, crying like I hadn't heard since Momma went to heaven. She finally stood back to look at him, and said, "Coleman, look at him. It's really him. Prayer really does work. I am so happy to see you, Dan. And look at you in a uniform. So you really are in the marines. Oh my god. Pete got a letter saying that you had graduated from Paris Island, South Carolina. We didn't know if it was you or some other Dan Bullock. Oh my god."

Dan said, "I did graduate. I sent you a letter too. But I sent it to the address on Elm Street. I will be here until I get my orders. I walked form the bus station, and I went through The Block. I saw Willie and Desi, and Desi told me that you had moved on the corner of Canal and Holt Street. Soon as I turned off Griffin Street, I saw Terry out there picking up pecans. I got as close as I could and told him to get back in that yard. He turned around so fast. It is good to be back home. I am going to stay down here for a few weeks or more, then I got to go to Brooklyn and see Gloria and Daddy. I will come back because my orders are going to mailed to Pete's house."

Lois was looking at Dan and rubbing his back, still crying. Then Lois said, "Let me call Pete and tell her you are here. I hope and pray that you will be all right. Are you hungry? There's some fried chicken, rice, and gravy, and some collard greens in the kitchen. Go and eat. I'm going to call Pete." Then she hugged him again and kissed his face on both sides.

Dan said, "Look at Chuckie, getting all big, with that pretty curly hair. Lois, he looks just like you. Reverend Coleman, I am glad to see you. I know you have been praying for me, and I want to thank you for that. Please keep me in your prayers, and my family too."

Reverend Coleman said, "Son, I always will. It's a blessing to see you. Now go on and get yourself something to eat. I know you are hungry. We'll talk later on, and you do know that you are welcome to stay here as long as you want too."

Dan said, "Yes, sir, Rev. Coleman. Thank you, sir."

Dan and I went into the kitchen, with Chuckie trailing behind. As Dan fixed his plate because we had already eaten. Before he could sit down, Lois called out, "Dan, come here! Pete is on the phone, and she don't believe you are really here. Come here and say something to her."

Dan got up and walked in the bedroom. I was following him as close as I could. Lois was sitting on the bed, handing Dan the telephone. Dan took the phone and said, "Hey, Pete, it's really me. I love you. How are you and the kids doing?" He was silent for a minute, then said, "Yeah, I know. I'm sorry, but I am all right. Come on so I can see you. Bring Tony and Gregory. I will be finished eating by the time you get here. Okay, I love you too. Come on, okay bye."

We went back in the kitchen, and Lois was still crying. She came in the kitchen with us and sat down at the table, watching Dan eat. Lois said, "Dan, I can't believe you are in the marines. How did you make it through boot camp, and what are you talking about waiting on your orders? Orders to do what, or to go where? I'm sorry. I just have so many questions. I still can't believe you are sitting here. We have been so worried about you. You look older, but you look good. Pete will be here shortly. Don't forget what I told you, you neither Terry." Lois went back in the living room with Reverend Coleman. Just as Dan finished eating, there was a loud knock at the door. We knew it was Aunt Pete,

Dan said, "Lois, let me get the door." Dan went to the door and said, "Who is it!"

Aunt Porter said, "Dan, you better open up this door right now. It's cold out here."

Dan opened the door, and they grabbed each other, hugging, and she was kissing his face. She was crying and saying, "Oh god! Oh god! Oh god! Dan, I've been so worried about you, especially since I got that letter. Look at you, in a uniform. So you really are in the marines. I thought they had the wrong Dan Bullock. Dan, you are too young to be in the marines. Tell me how you get in there?"

Dan stepped back, looked at her, and said, "I got my birth certificate before I went to Brooklyn, and I just wanted to go in the army, and I took an ink pen and blotted out the original birth date. I wiped it off, and I told the recruiter that the lady in the clerk's office did it. I didn't think he would go for it, but he told me I had to take some tests, so I did. Except he told me I had to go in the marines because my test scores weren't high enough to go in the army."

Pete said, "Dan, don't you know that a war is going on over in Vietnam? You got grown men trying to evade the draft by going to Canada and getting into colleges. And here you are, still fourteen years old, or young, I should say. I can't believe this. It ain't right. Dan, I am so scared for you. You promise me that if they try to send you to Vietnam, tell them how old you really are. That way, they will put you out. But at least you won't be in no war, and you'll be alive. But you do look so handsome in that uniform, and you look taller and older. But you are still a fourteen-year-old boy, Dan."

Dan was looking at her the whole time. When she seemed to have finished her speech, Dan said, "Pete, I am a marine now. I know that I'm only fourteen, but I am a man now. And when I get my orders, if they send me to Vietnam, then I'm going. I want to fight for my country, and if it comes to it, I will die for my country. Just keep me in prayer, if I do go over to Vietnam. I will write y'all every week. I would only be over there for a year, and it will go by fast. I will be back before you know it. Besides, I might not even go to Vietnam. I might go to Germany, or even somewhere else. Wherever I go, I will be praying like Reverend Coleman told me, and I know that y'all will be praying for me too."

Pete walked up to Dan, put her hands on both sides of his face, she kissed him, and said, "Dan, I'm going to always pray for you, and I will always love you too. So I'm not going to be thinking negative.

You are going to be just fine, and you will come back home to us. You better write too! Lois, look at him in his uniform. But Dan, you don't need to be wearing that uniform around. It ain't everybody's business. You got anymore clothes?"

Dan jumped around and headed for the back door, saying, "I forgot my duffle bag on the back porch." When Dan came back inside, he said, "Yes, I stopped on my way from the bus station and bought some jeans, shirts, and a heavy coat with a hood on it, so I will put my uniform up while I am here Pete."

Pete said, "Dan, it's so good to see you and to have you back home. I hope your orders don't ever come so you can stay here with us. But when they come, I hope it's in Hawaii."

Everyone started laughing…

We all enjoyed Dan until he had to go to Brooklyn. He had everyone's telephone number, so we all felt good about that. And knowing that he had to come back when his orders came in the mail at Pete's house. But still, it was a sad day when he left on the bus; we watched until the bus was out of sight.

CHAPTER 13

Night Stalking/Easter Weekend

Dan had been gone to Brooklyn for a long time, but he called from a telephone booth every few days. He called Aunt Pete to talk to her, Tony, and Greg. He would always ask her if his orders had come in. He would call Lois too, and I would get to speak to him, so would Chuckie. Sometimes, Dan would talk to Reverend Coleman, but he spent most of the time talking to Lois. On this one night, she got really excited and told us that Dan might be coming back home early. That meant he would be here for Easter. I knew that Reverend Coleman wanted him to be here so he could attend church on Easter Sunday. Lois was so happy that he was coming.

When she hung the phone up, she said, "Terry, Chuckie, Dan might be back sooner than I thought. He might be here for Easter Sunday."

"I will be glad to see him. Chuckie will too," I said.

Later that day, Lois was talking to Aunt Pete, and she was saying, "Well, Dan said Gloria Jean is doing okay. And Daddy is working, doing alright. And you know Dan don't ever mention Jewel. I know he doesn't like her. None of us do."

Then Pete said, "Well, I couldn't stand her, but it's not her fault. So I don't even give her the thought of day. Daddy is the one I was upset at, but just like with her, I don't even give him the thought of the day either. I told Dan to make sure that Gloria has our telephone numbers and to call us. She knows we are here for her, but she is the baby and loves her daddy. The only time we are going to see her is if we go up there, or Daddy brings her down here to visit. I wish Dan would bring her with him when he comes back. But Daddy ain't about to let her come down here without him. He won't let nothing happen to her. She will be all right."

Lois said, "I told Dan to call me tomorrow and have Gloria with him so I can talk to her. He said he will try. I don't know why he has to try unless Daddy don't want her talking to us."

Pete said, "Well, I better get back home before it gets too late. I got to go to work in that door factory early in the morning and get Tony us for school. So take care. Tell Reverend Coleman I said hello when he comes home. You better be good to him. He's a man of God."

"I will. Good night. Terry, you and Chuckie, get ready to go take your baths. Terry, you go first. I will give Chuckie one when you finish," said Lois.

When the telephone started to ring, Lois picked it up before I could get to it. She said, "Hello, Coleman residence. What! Are you serious? When! Well, when you get here, catch a cab from the bus station. What about Gloria? Oh, okay. Well, you tell her that we all love her. Did you give her our telephone numbers? Well, we will be glad to see you, you know that, Dan. Call Pete and let her know that you are coming. Terry is standing right here, looking in my mouth, so speak to him before you hang up. Here, Terry."

I grabbed the phone, smiling from ear to ear and said, "Hey, Dan, Momma said you are coming back home. When?"

Dan said, "I am leaving tomorrow. I will go to the Transport Authority in the city in the morning and get my bus ticket. The bus will leave at eleven o'clock. I might be there by dinnertime, so don't eat up all the food."

I started laughing and said, "You know I'm not going to eat up all the food. Dan, what is the Transport Authority?"

Dan said, "Well, that's the biggest bus station that I have ever seen, and all kinds of people are in and out of there. People from all across the world: real Africans and White people from Ireland, Italy, and other countries too. I just look at all the people passing by, while I wait for the bus. Well, I got to go now. I will see you tomorrow. Be good."

I said, "Okay, I will see you tomorrow. I will be waiting. Bye, Dan."

After hanging the phone up, I went and told Chuckie that Dan was coming back home tomorrow. He was just smiling; he loved Dan.

Reverend Coleman was sitting in the living room, reading his Bible. I went in there and said, "Reverend Coleman, Dan is coming back home tomorrow. I talked to him on the phone earlier today."

Reverend Coleman looked up from his Bible, smiling, and he said, "That's good, son. Hopefully he will be here for Easter next week. That way, he can attend church with all of us on Easter Sunday. Did he say about what time he will get here?"

I said, "Yes, sir. He said he will be here by dinnertime. He is going to the Port Authority in the morning, and his bus leaves at eleven o'clock. He said save him some dinner too."

Reverend Coleman said, "I will make sure he has more than enough to eat when he gets here, so don't worry about that. I want you to go out there and chop some wood. It's going to get a little cold tonight. Just cut enough to last through the night and to cook with tomorrow. Let Chuckie help you bring it inside. He's old enough to help out a little."

I said, "Yes, sir," then went and got Chuckie. I walked to the back porch where Chuckie was playing with a water pistol and said, "Come on, Chuckie, we are going outside, and you can help me chop wood. I will chop it, and then you can take some inside and put them on the stack, okay?"

"Okay," said Chuckie, eager to help his big brother.

It was a nice warm day in April; the sun was shining, and the breeze was calm. The fig trees were ready to be picked again. I knew that they came out in the late summer and early fall, but Reverend

Coleman told me that they have two crops of fruit because they grow during the winter and are ready in the beginning of Spring.

I said, "Come on, Chuckie. Let's get some of those figs and eat them before we start chopping the wood."

I reached up and got two of the figs and handed Chuckie one of them. Chuckie could reach the figs; he was going to turn six next month on the eighth. So when I started to chop wood, he noticed that Chuckie was still over at the fig tree. After he had chopped enough wood for the night and for tomorrow, he called Chuckie to come and help take the wood in the house. He never talked much, so I was surprised when he said, "Terry, why Momma and Aunt Pete say Dan is too young to be in the marines?"

I looked down at him and said, "He is in the marines. You saw his uniform. So what they say doesn't matter because it won't change anything. When he get his orders to leave, he will go wherever they want him to go. I am just glad that he is coming back home before he leaves to start active duty in the marines. He will be here tomorrow, I know you will be glad to see him too."

Chuckie stopped eating his fig long enough to say, "Yeah, I will."

The next morning, everyone seemed to be on edge, awaiting for the arrival of Dan. It was Saturday, so Momma didn't have to work. She called the bus station and found out the bus from New York was due in at four thirty-five in the evening. Dan called from the Port Authority that morning and said he was about to leave. Aunt Pete, Tony, and Greg came over about three thirty to wait for Dan. Aunt Pete was talking to Momma on the front porch, when I went around there. She was saying, "We ought to go to the bus station and meet him."

Lois said, "He is going to catch a cab. He'll be here. Terry, go back around and look out for those children. I told you about that eavesdropping. Keep on. You are going to get a whooping."

I said, "Well, what time is it?"

"It's time for you to go in the backyard with Tony and them. Go ahead on now!" said Lois.

When I got in the backyard, Tony and Chuckie was racing. Tony was way out in front of Chuckie. Tony could run fast, like Aunt Pete. No one could outrun Aunt Pete; she could outrun the boys. I ran from her one time, and she gave me a half block and caught me before I could get to the end of the block. Tony and Greg probably were going to be real fast just like she is. I never saw Momma race or run, except maybe a few feet. Dan was the only one who could keep up with Aunt Pete; he might beat her now since he is a marine. Besides, Dan is bigger and older now. I could beat Tony, only because I was older than him by two years. They all went and sit on the back porch, talking about who was the fastest. I went into the house and got some water and glasses and gave them some water to drink.

Tony said, "Terry, when is Dan coming? We've been waiting all day long."

I said, "I just asked Momma what time it was. She said it was three thirty, and his bus is supposed to be here at four thirty. So it won't be long now."

We were on the back porch, trying to see who could jump off the porch the farthest. Just as I was getting ready to jump, Dan walked out of the back door.

Dan said, "Don't mind me, go on and jump, Terry."

We all ran to him at one time; everyone trying to hug him. Lois and Aunt Pete came outside. They were just looking at us, with a smile on their faces. Dan looked better than when we first saw him before he left. We all sat outside until it started to get dark. Aunt Pete told Tony and Greg to get ready to go. She then said, "Dan, we are getting ready to leave now, but come over in the morning, and I will make breakfast for you, okay?"

Dan said, "I will be there, and we will walk y'all to the corner. Come on, Terry and Chuckie."

As we walked, Dan and Aunt Porter were talking to each other. We ran ahead, and when we got to the corner, we waited for them to catch up. When they got to the corner, they hugged, and Aunt Porter said goodnight.

When we got back, Momma said, "Dan, y'all come on in the kitchen so you can eat. I asked Pete if she and the children wanted to stay for dinner, but she cooked before she came over here." She knew Dan was coming, so she cooked his favorite meal: fried chicken, rice and gravy, and collard greens, with some corn bread. She even made a chocolate cake, which was all our favorite cake. Then she sat down after fixing her plate and said, "Y'all bow your heads. Dear heavenly Father, we come to you in prayer, thanking you for your many blessings and asking for your continuous mercy. And dear God, we ask that you bless this food that we are about to eat for the nourishment of our bodies. And dear God, please bless and protect Dan no matter where is goes and keep him safe from all hurt, harm, and danger. We ask in the name of Jesus Christ, amen. Okay, let's eat."

Dan looked like he was about to cry, then he got up and went over to Lois and hugged her neck, kissed her on the face, telling her that he loved her. Then she looked like she was going to cry. After we ate, Lois and Dan were in the kitchen, washing dishes and talking. We were in the living room, when Reverend Coleman came in. He went into the kitchen with Dan and Momma and joined the conversation. I helped Chuckie with his coloring book, waiting for a chance to talk to Dan. Then they all moved to the living room and continued their conversation. Reverend Coleman, Momma, and Dan were still in the living room, talking when we went to bed.

The next morning, when I woke up, Dan was gone. Then I remembered that he was going to go over Aunt Pete's house for breakfast. Reverend Coleman and Lois were in the kitchen; he was drinking coffee, while she fixed breakfast. Chuckie was already in the kitchen eating eggs, grits, and bacon. After washing up and brushing my teeth, I headed toward the kitchen. That's when I heard Dan come in the back door. I could see he had on sweatpants and a sweatshirt, and that he was sweating and breathing hard.

I said, "Dan, I thought you went over to Aunt Pete's house to eat breakfast. I didn't know you were out jogging. I could have gone with you."

Dan said, "I have to run to stay in shape and to stay conditioned. I ran all the way to the Truck Lane and back. I started to do it again. I am going to wash up so I can go around Pete's house. When

I come back, we will go downtown, and I am going to buy us a suit for Easter, all right?"

"Reverend Coleman is going to buy me a suit," I said.

Dan said, "I told him that I would buy your suit this year. He is going to get Chuckie a suit. We'll get a suit just alike, the same color. What color do you want to get?"

"I want to get a blue suit and a blue tie to go with it. I want some new shoes too. Are you gonna be able to buy me some new shoes?" I asked.

Dan started laughing and said, "I sure will, and some socks too. All right, let me wash off so I can get going."

Later on that day, Dan and I walked downtown. We avoided The Block by going down Alabama Avenue until we got to Mulberry Street. While walking, I asked a thousand questions. I asked, "Dan, did they teach you how to shoot a real gun, like the twenty-two rifle Granddaddy gave you for your birthday that time?"

Dan said, "I learned to shoot a M16. It is an automatic weapon. I learned how to take it apart and put it back together. That was the easiest part. We had to march with heavy equipment on our backs for five whole miles. It was really hard, and even painful. This guy from Brooklyn named McArthur, he looked out for me because he thought I was from Brooklyn. But some of the guys from Brooklyn or the Bronx didn't think I was from Brooklyn because of the way I talked or sounded. Anyway, I made it through basic training. That was the hardest part. And I will make it through my tour of duty wherever I go. Come on, we can talk about that later."

We went to Edwards Young Men's Shop, the most expensive clothing store in Goldsboro.

I said, "Dan, all these suit costs a lot of money. These are the best suits people can buy."

Dan said, "Well, we are going to get the best that money can buy. That's why we came here. Don't worry, the marines pay me good money, Terry. Hey, sir, can we get some assistance over here. We both want to purchase the best blue suits that you have in here, sir."

Then that man showed us the blue suits, and Dan picked both of our suits out. We tried them on to make sure they fit us. Then we tried on our new shoes, and they fit perfectly. Dan then asked if he could use the phone to call a cab. While we waited for the cab, Dan went over to the socks and picked out a light-blue and dark-blue pair for me and the same for him. So we rode the cab back home.

Easter Sunday came so fast. Momma had on a pretty light-blue dress, and Reverend Coleman was dressed in his usual signature black suit, white shirt, and black tie. Dan, Chuckie, and I had on royal-blue suits, white shirts, and blue ties. Momma wanted Chuckie to dress like us. I knew that Momma wanted Chuckie to have a suit the color of ours because I heard her ask Dan what color suit he was going to buy us. When Reverend Pate came to pick us up in his new gray Buick, Reverend Coleman got in the front, and we got in the back. Dan put Chuckie on his lap. I was in the middle, and Momma was right behind Reverend Coleman by the window. She warned me and Dan and told us not to mention that Dan was in the marines. We both told her that we understood.

The people at the church were very nice. Everyone seemed to be speaking to Reverend Coleman and Reverend Pate when we got out of the car. We went inside and sat on the front row. Dan handed me two dollars and said, "When they pass the plate around, put it in the plate. Lois said you will fall asleep, so I want you to stay awake, okay, Terry?"

"Yes, I will," I said.

The choir was singing "How Great Thou Art." (*Oh Lord, my God. When I, in awesome wonder, consider all the worlds thy hands have made. I see the stars; I hear the rolling thunder. Thy power throughout the universe displayed. Then sings my soul, my Savior God to thee. How great thou art, how great thou art.*]

Lois leaned over and said, "Dan, take Chuckie to the rest room so he can pee and take Terry too so he will stay awake."

Dan said, "Okay, I got them. Come on, Terry."

Dan picked Chuckie up, and we went down the hallway to the bathroom. When we came back, Reverend Coleman was at the podium, saying, "We all know that today is Easter Sunday, which Jesus's resurrection. After Jesus was crucified on that dreadful Friday, his body was taken down from the cross and buried in a cave tomb.

The tomb was guarded by Roman soldiers and a big, huge stone was placed over the front of the entrance. And then on Sunday, Mary Magdalene and some of Jesus's disciples visited the tomb. When they got there, they found out that the big stone had been moved, and the body of Jesus was no longer there. And Jesus was seen later that day by Mary and the disciples and, for forty days afterward, by many other people. His followers realized that the Almighty God had raised Jesus from the dead. We Christians call this the resurrection. And we believe that through his resurrection, Jesus overcame death and sin. This offers people the promise of eternal life if they follow his teachings. I am here to tell you that we serve a living God through Christ Jesus. He is the same today that he was then. Read your Bible. The Bible was written by men who were inspired by God. The Bible is God's word. And as I've said many times before, some books were written to inform you, and some books were written to reform you, but only the Bible was written to transform you. And with this, I will turn it over to Reverend Pate." Reverend Coleman stepped back as people started clapping and praising the Lord.

Some of the congregation started to walk out because they were the ones who was going to prepare the food. We always ate after church. After Reverend Pate started speaking, I fell asleep because Dan was waking me up, telling me it was time to go outside and eat.

Everyone was dressed in their new suits, dresses, and shiny shoes. Momma and Dan got our plates, and we went to a table set up outside. Reverend Coleman joined us shortly thereafter; people kept coming up to him, shaking his hand, and the ladies giving him hugs. Momma was on edge because she didn't like the ladies hugging on him.

Finally, she said, "Come on y'all. Let's go. Coleman, get Chuckie." She then walked over to Reverend Pate and said something to him, and he went to the car as she stood there, waiting for us to catch up. We got into the car and left.

When we got home, we all changed out of our Sunday clothes. Dan said, "Let's walk around Pete's house, then over to Aunt Bents and Aunt Agnus for a few minutes."

As we started to walk off, Chuckie came running behind us, and Momma said, "Dan, take Chuckie with you. He wants to see Greg and Reggie. Tell Pete to give baby Rodney a kiss for me."

Dan said, "Okay, I will tell her." Dan held Chuckies hand so he wouldn't lag behind.

When we approached Persimmon Street, a girl said, "Hey, Dan, it's nice to see you. Where have you been? I haven't seen you in a long time. I heard you were in New York."

Dan said, "Hey, Patricia, it's nice to see you too. Yeah, I live in Brooklyn now. I am just here visiting. That's your baby sister? What's her name? Sharon?"

Patricia said, "I know your sister Lois told you her name. She looks just like Terry, don't she?"

Dan looked at Terry and said, "Yeah, they look just like Desi."

I heard them talking, and when I heard my name, I said, "Dan, what you say about me? Who do I look like?"

Dan said, "You look like Desi Atkinson, your daddy, and that little girl Sharon too. But you are a Bullock, so don't worry about it. Come on, Chuckie, let's go y'all. Bye, Patricia."

Chuck said, "Sharon is pretty, ain't she, Terry?"

I looked back, and Sharon was looking at me, and her other two sisters walked up to her, and was looking at us. Faye was in my class at school, and the other girl's name was Butt. I played marbles with their brother James. Momma didn't want me going down there to play with them. She said their daddy didn't want me down there, so I never went anymore.

When we got to Aunt Porter's house, Bill was outside, on the porch, still in his charcoal gray suit and tie. He was talking to Reggie, Greg, and Tony. Rodney was in the house with Aunt Porter. Tony, Greg, and Reggie ran up to Dan before we could get in the yard. They were happy to see him. Reggie was the first one reach to Dan; he was very fast. He could outrun boys older than he was, and he was always smiling. He loved everybody, and everybody loved him. Greg was kind of quiet and very smart. Tony acted mature for his age and even acted like Dan.

Aunt Porter came outside, holding Rodney in her arms. She said, "Hey, Dan, how are y'all doing? I was wondering when you were going to come around. I got a letter for you yesterday in the mail. Tony, go in there and look on my dresser and get that envelope and bring it out here. The rest of y'all go play somewhere, not you, Terry."

Tony came back with the letter, and Aunt Porter told him to give it to Dan. He opened the letter and read it. Then he said, "I have to be back at Camp Lejeune on Wednesday. I guess my orders have come in. Bill, I need about ten dollars. I spent my money on our Easter suits. I will let you have my watch."

Bill said, "Dan, I will give you ten dollars, but you keep your watch. Are you sure that's all you need?"

Dan said, "Yeah, that's all I need Bill, thanks. I will pay you when I come back."

Bill said, "Don't you worry about that. You just take care of yourself, and don't forget our phone number."

Dan said, "I won't forget. Well, Pete, I love you, and you take care. I hope I get to stay at Camp Lejeune so I can come home on weekends. I will call and let y'all know what's going on. Terry, get Chuckie, and let's go. I will be back by here before I leave, Pete."

"Okay, Dan. You take care of yourself, and don't trust nobody. Don't let them know how old you really are unless they try to send you to Vietnam. God bless you," said Pete.

When we got back home, Dan went into the living room with Momma and Reverend Coleman. Then Momma came in and took Chuckie in the bathroom, saying, "Terry, you are next, so get ready to take your bath. Rocky finally went to sleep, and I am tired. I got to work tomorrow, so y'all are going to bed early tonight too. There's no school tomorrow, so Dan will be here to look after y'all."

I said, "Yes, ma'am."

I could then hear Reverend Coleman telling Dan, "Son, don't you worry. Your birth certificate says you are eighteen, and now you are nineteen. Just keep your secret to yourself, and if things get too hard, do like Pete told you. And just let them know that you are only fifteen years old and come on back home. It won't be nothing to be shame about."

Dan said, "Reverend Coleman, I already been through the hard part. I will be all right. I want to make sure that Gloria is going to be all right, and Lois and Pete too. Like you said, I will pray and trust in Jesus. God will take care of me, and you will keep me in prayer too."

Lois said, "Terry, come on and get in the bathtub. I cleaned it out, and the water is running, so hurry up. Don't let that water run over. Come on, Chuckie, and let's get your pajama's on so you can get in bed."

The next day seemed to blur by. We spent most of the day talking. But I noticed that Dan was becoming less talkative. He seemed to be daydreaming a lot. I guess he was thinking. But he looked sad, so I asked, "Dan, what's wrong with you? Why are you looking like that?"

Dan just smiled and said, "I'm all right. I was just thinking, and a lot of times when I get quiet, I just be praying, that's all. Sometimes, I think back to boot camp and wondered how I made it through, even with the help of a few friends. Promise me that if you go into the military, or Tony, any of you, wait until you are eighteen years old and make sure you get in the best shape you can be in before you even sign up for it. Because it just might be the hardest physical thing you will ever do in life.

"Anyway, we need a flashlight and a tow sack. We are gonna go over on Miller Street and go up in the attic in that two-story house on the corner. That's where the pigeons go to roost at night. I saw them out on that house when we come from Aunt Bent's house yesterday, and they usually sleep where they hang out at. It was a lot of them, and they stick together, so it should be a lot of them together. The flashlight will temporarily blind them, and we can catch them and put some of them in the tow sack."

I asked, "Dan, what are we gonna do with them if we catch them? Let them go?"

Dan started laughing and said, "We are going to do them like Momma use to do the chickens, and then pluck and cook them. This is how you will learn how to survive if you need too. Come on. Let's get a sack, and I will ask Reverend Coleman for a flashlight."

As we walked down Holt Street toward Miller Steet, I said, "Dan, I'm not gonna eat no pigeon. I don't care who cooks it."

Dan laughed and said, "We'll it will be more for me to eat, but it tastes just like chicken. But the whole reason for all this is so we can spend time together and for you to learn a survival skill. You don't have to eat it. We're here let's go in the back door. We got to be careful. This is an old house."

"Okay," I said, feeling relieved for not having to eat a pigeon.

Dan was shining the flashlight, as we approached the steps. The back door was ajar, so he just pushed it open wide so we could get inside without touching it or getting our clothes dirty. The house had been empty for a long time; dust was everywhere. We went through the kitchen upon entry. The flashlight made it seem as if shadows was off in the corners moving around. Broken furniture was laying around in the two rooms that we went through. And when we got to the steps, the first seven steps were broken and rotten on the outside. Dan climbed on the left, and when he got into a stable position, he reached down and grabbed my wrist and pulled me up. We had no problem the rest of the way. When we got to the second floor, there was a chair. The chair was missing a leg. We could see in the attic because Dan shined the flashlight on the square hole in the ceiling.

Dan pulled the chair under the hole in the ceiling and said, "Terry, you hold this side of the chair so I can jump up and grab the top. When I get up there, I will get a few pigeons and put them in the sack, tie it up, and throw it down to you."

I held the chair as best I could, and when Dan jumped, he grabbed the inside of the square hold. Dan yelled really loud and came crashing down. One of his feet hit the chair, and the other hit the floor. When he fell on the floor, he quickly got up, holding his hand. He said, "I grabbed a nail and cut my hand." His right hand was bleeding profusely, and he took his T-shirt off and wrapped it around his hand. We went down the steps; when he got to the broken part, he jumped. Then when I got to the broken part, he told me to jump. I jumped and he caught me, and we left out and went home.

When we got home, Lois was on the front porch with Reverend Coleman. Dan tried to go pass and go into the back door. Lois said, "Dan, come here! What's wrong with your hand? You got your T-shirt around your hand, and I see the blood. What happened?" Dan told her what happened and said he would be all right. Then Lois said, "Come on in here so I can clean it up. I have some peroxide, salve, and bandages. You went all through boot camp and didn't get a scratch. Come home and get your hand all cut up. You better be careful and take care of yourself."

They went into the bathroom, and when they came out, Lois said, "It's not as bad as I thought it was. Just keep working it so it won't get stiff. You are leaving in the morning. Here's twenty dollars to take with you. Bill will be here to take me to work, then he will drop you off at the bus station."

The next morning, I was on the front porch with Chuckie and Reverend Coleman as Dan and Momma was about to leave.

Dan hugged me and said, "I will be back soon. You look out for your brothers and cousins and Lois and Pete too. Reverend Coleman, please keep me in your prayers."

Reverend Coleman said, "I will, son. Don't forget the Serenity Prayer I taught you. Take care of yourself and trust in the Lord always."

Dan put his duffel bag on the back seat and climbed inside, waving at us as the car pulled off. We watched until the car turned onto Pine Street. Not knowing that the next time I see him, he would be in a casket, with a glass top over it.

CHAPTER 14

Orders for Active Duty: Vietnam

It was several weeks before Momma got a call from Dan; we knew it was Dan because she told everyone to be quiet. Then Momma said, "Yes, I'll accept. Hello, Dan, I am glad to hear from you. How are doing? What! When? Oh my god, I still can't believe this is really happening. Are you sure you want to go through with this?" She listened for moment or two before saying, "Well okay, I won't say anything. Do you know when you are leaving? That's not long, so you are going to leave on the fifth and get there on the eighth? Yeah, he's right here. Come here, Terry. Dan wants to speak to you. Don't hang up. I want to talk to him again, okay?"

I said, "Okay, Momma. Hey, Dan, where are you going and when are you coming back home?"

Dan while laughing said, "Terry, I know that you got a lot of questions, but slow down little, bruh. Well, I got my orders today, that's why I'm calling. I am going to Vietnam in a less than two weeks, and I will be over there for about a year. But the time will go by so fast, and I will be back home before you know it. And just like Bill told me, I got to think positive and not negative. That's what I want you to do too. I will write to Lois, and I will tell her to let you read my letters so you will hear from me, and I want you to look out for Tony, Chuckie, Greg, Rocky, and Reggie. Be good and listen to Lois, Pete, Bill, Reverend Coleman, and your teachers. And I want you to stay smart, keep getting good grades because I am going to see your report card when I come back home, okay? Let me speak back to Lois."

Momma talked to Dan for a few more minutes and hanged the phone up. Reverend Coleman was listening the entire time, and when Momma sit down, he said, "Lois, he is going to be just fine. Don't worry."

"I sure hope so, Coleman, but I had no idea he would use his birth certificate to enlist in the marines. I only meant for him to be able to get a job so he could take care of himself. Jewel got a lot of children, and I know she doesn't even want none of Daddy's children up there. He could have always come back home, if I had to go up there and get him myself. But I can't go all the way over to Vietnam to get him. Lord, I hope I don't end up hating myself. God forbid if anything should happen to him, I would never forgive myself. Why is Terry calling me? Let me go see what he wants," said Lois. Lois got up and went to the front door and saw Pete and Bill getting out of the car with the children.

As Aunt Porter was walking up the steps with Reggie in her arms, Momma reached for Reggie, who always seem to be happy and smiling. Momma said, "Give him to me, with his pretty self. He's too pretty to be a boy. Hey, Tony and Greg, I am happy to see y'all. Come on inside. I got some sweet potato pie and some Kool-Aid in the kitchen. Bill, how are you doing? Come on in the living room. Come on, Pete, and don't be trying to rush off."

We all went into the kitchen, except Bill; he went into the living room where Reverend Coleman was sitting reading his Bible.

Aunt Pete was telling Momma that she and Bill had talked to Dan too. Momma gave us all a piece of potato pie and a glass of grape Kool-Aid. We were all quiet, listening to Aunt Pete. She was saying, "Well, it might be a year before we see Dan again. Bill was telling me that if a family has only one boy in it, that he can't even go in the military. And all those grown men, especially the rich ones, are doing all they can to evade going into the military. Girl, that makes me so mad. Dan told me that Aunt Leatha told him that she was going to call the Red Cross and tell them that he is only fourteen years old. He said he told her that if she did, he would wait until he was eighteen and reenlist. She told him if he was that determined to go, she won't say anything. I sure hope and pray that he will be all right."

Lois said, "Well, he survived basic training, and we all just have to keep praying that he will survive Vietnam. Coleman told me that it seems every week men are being killed at an alarming rate. That scares me to my heart, and I don't know even understand why America is over there fighting those people in the first place."

Aunt Porter said, "Well, Bill be keeping up with what's going on over in Vietnam as best as he can. You know he was a paratrooper in the army, and he spent a lot of time talking to Dan. I know he is very concerned too, mainly because of all the deaths over there. Every night on the *World News*, all they talk about is how many marines or soldiers got killed. Girl, you are married to a preacher, and we all got to keep Dan in our prayers."

Momma said, "Come on, let's go in the living room. Terry, put those saucers in the sink. I will wash them later. Y'all come on so we can all join hands and pray for Dan."

As we walked into the living room, Uncle Bill was saying, "More marines are getting killed in Vietnam every day. About 1 out of every 10 of all those serving over there are getting killed. Just a few years ago in 1967, I think it was on July 28, 1967, I should have brought that article with me, but the *Star News* reported in the week before 164 Americans had been killed in Vietnam and over a thousand wounded. And that put the death toll in the war over 12,000, and over 70,000 wounded, and over 600 missing or captured. When General Westmoreland was in charge over there, he had complete control of how he did things. He seemed to only be concerned about the body count. He used search and destroy tactics just to measure the body counts. As long as more Vietnamese was being killed than Americans, he felt he was winning the war. I don't even believe he cared anything about stopping communism. I think it was all about the body count. I am glad that Westmoreland is no longer the general over there. They got a four-star general named Creighton Abraham, or Abrams, something like that. He did away with that search and destroy tactic and started securing and holding populated areas. But war is war, and death is imminent in war. But still, it gives me more hope that Dan will return home alive and in one piece."

Aunt Porter said, "Lois, I told you Bill be keeping up with what's going on over there. He is a soldier for life. Dan is going to be a marine for life too. Terry, Tony, Greg, y'all hold hands. Come here, Reggie. Give me your hand, baby. Everybody, hold hands. Reverend Coleman, will you pray for Dan?"

Reverend Coleman said, "I sure will. Everyone, bow your heads. Dear Heavenly Father, we come together in the name of Jesus Christ. Dear Heavenly Father, in Matthew 18:19–20, your word tells us that, 'Again I say unto you, that if two of you shall agree on earth as touching anything that they shall ask, it shall be done for them of my Father who is in Heaven. For where two or three are gathered together in my name, there am I in the midst of them.' Dear Heavenly Father, we are gathered here today, with love and concern for our loved one, Dan Bullock. And Lord, as you already know the circumstances, we are here today to ask you in accordance to your word, and we pray that you, oh Lord, will Bless and protect Dan Bullock as he goes on his journey overseas to Vietnam. We ask in the name of Jesus Christ that you will put a hedge around him, oh Lord. Dear Heavenly Father, Dan is like a David going up against a Goliath at his young and tender age. He is a boy among men, with the opposition intending on taking his precious life. We know how you protected David, and we pray and ask that you will do the same thing for Dan Bullock. We claim your victory right now, today. and days to come until you bring Dan back home safely. In the name of Jesus Christ, we thank you, we love you, and bless your holy name. And now Heavenly Father, as you have taught us to pray, everyone join in, please. Our Father, who art in heaven, hallowed be thy name, thy kingdom come, thy will be done in earth as it is in heaven. Give us this day our daily bread. And forgive us our trespasses as we forgive them that trespass against us. And lead us not into temptation, but deliver us from evil. For thine is the kingdom, the power, and the glory. For ever and ever. Amen."

Lois said, "Dan is going to be all right. I know God heard our prayers. Pete, did you hear Tony and Terry reciting the Lord's Prayer? Greg and Chuckie too? I am so proud of y'all."

Pete said, "Oh yeah, we always pray with them before they go to bed at night, and Bill have been teaching them the Lord's Prayer for years now, and you know that they say the Lord's Prayer in school too. And they know the Lord hears their prayers, just like he hears ours. Reverend Coleman, thank you so very much for taking the time to pray for Dan."

While giving Reverend Coleman a hug, he said, "It was my pleasure, Pete. We will always keep Dan in our prayers. I had a long talk with him about Jesus, and he is a child of God. He accepted Jesus in his life, and we can only pray that it is God's will that Dan will be back home with us sooner than later."

When Aunt Porter was leaving, she said to Uncle Bill, "I sure hope Dan don't come back too soon. Reverend Coleman messed me up when he said that 'if it's God's will, that Dan will be back sooner than later.' I'm just going to rebuke that statement in the name of Jesus. Tony, you and Greg, get in the back seat so we can go home. Bye, Terry and Chuckie. Y'all be good now. Love y'all."

As I held the door open for Tony and Greg, Uncle Bill said, "You do understand that everything happens according to God's will. He didn't mean no harm. All right, Terry and Chuckie, we'll see y'all tomorrow. Take care."

We stood in the front yard and watched them leave. Tony was waving through the back window. After they turned onto Persimmons Street, we went back into the house.

CHAPTER 15

———

Homecoming: The Legacy Begins

On May 8, 1969, it was a beautiful Thursday morning. The sun was shining, and birds seemed to be singing happy birthday to Chuckie—for he was turning seven years old today and could hardly wait for this day to come. That's when I realized Momma was singing happy birthday to Chuckie, and then she said, "Terry, we are going to celebrate Prentice Ray Coleman's birthday today. He is seven years old today. That means no school today, so get washed up, dressed up because we are going to go downtown and shop for Chuckie's birthday present. Chuckie, do you know what you want for your birthday?"

Chuckie looked at Terry and said, "I want some All-Stars like Terry got, only I want the black ones, please?"

Lois said, "Terry has both colors, white and black. So why don't we get you both colors, white and black. What do you think about that, birthday boy?"

Chuckie was smiling from ear to ear and said, "Momma, I wear a size seven, and I'm seven years old today. Thanks, Momma."

"You know you're welcome, baby," said Lois.

As we were eating breakfast, Momma said, "We'll, today is also the day that Dan arrived in Vietnam. I sure wish he was home with

145

us to help celebrate your birthday, Chuckie. I still can't believe he is in the marines. And now he's somewhere halfway across the world, getting ready to fight for his country and his young life. I'm about like Pete now. They don't care nothing about him. He is just another body over there. We just got to keep him in our prayers and pray that he comes back home to us in one piece."

I asked, "Momma, why everybody keep saying that they wish Dan comes back in one piece."

Momma said, "Because some people come back with one arm, or with one leg. They don't come back with their whole body. Some come back with their whole body, but part of their mind be missing. And they don't never be the same again. Their families don't even know them anymore and even turn against them. The family don't even want them coming around them anymore. The war can change a grown man, and I am afraid of what it can do to Dan. He just turned fifteen years old. He just looks and acts older, but he's still a child. But it's in God's hands now. All we can do is pray for him. We won't ever turn away from Dan, no matter what. I know that Pete won't ever turn away from him either. We just want him to come back home to us. Daddy broke our family up by leaving Momma for that Jewel woman and getting married to her. But me and Pete made a vow to always keep the rest of our family together. Terry, you and Chuckie, go on and get dressed while I call a cab. We'll be ready by the time he gets here. I should call Desi, but we will ride up to The Block and walk the rest of the way if we don't see Desi. Don't worry, we will catch a cab back home."

We all got into the cab and left for the block.

When we got on The Block, Momma told the cab driver to drop us off at Doris's house. Doris was my daddy's niece, so Momma told me that Doris was my first cousin. I saw my daddy's black Cadillac parked on the side of her house. Momma knocked on the door and opened the screen door at the same time. She said, "Hey, Doris, how you are doing?"

Doris was an extremely beautiful woman, with a light complexion, just like Terry and Desi. Her hair was long, black and silky. She looked up and said, "Hey, Lois, Desi walked over to the poolroom to get some money from somebody that owes him. He said he'd be right back, and look at Terry, looking just like my uncle John Desi Atkinson. Come here with your curly haired self and give me a hug, baby."

Terry went over to her and gave her a hug, telling her that it was Chuckie's birthday.

She said, "Chuckie, you come on over here and let me give you a birthday hug and a dollar too, looking like Lois, with all that curly hair."

Chuckie went over to her, and she handed him a dollar and hugged him. He quickly went back to Momma.

Doris said, "Lois, do Reverend Coleman know that you are up here? Girl, you know you are married now."

Momma said, "I go where I want to go. He doesn't tell me what to do. But I do love him. He's a good man. I can come see you when I get ready. There's no harm in that. He knows that I ain't studying Desi no more." Momma turned around suddenly at the sound of the loud knocking!

Momma looked at the door at the same time Doris did, and Doris said, "That's Desi. Come on in, Uncle Desi."

He was tall and very handsome and also very married. Momma couldn't take her eyes off him. He was looking straight at Terry, and Terry was looking back at him. Desi said, "Doris, look at my boy, looking just like me. Lois, how is he doing?"

Lois said, "He is doing just fine. He can talk. Why don't you ask him? Look how he is looking at you, Desi."

I said, "I know you are my daddy, and Doris is my cousin. But I am still a Bullock, just like Dan."

Lois said, "You tell him, baby!" then she started laughing, so did Doris and Desi. Then Lois said, "Desi, take us downtown. It's Chuckie's birthday, and I am going to buy him some All-Stars."

Desi said, "Sure, I will. Are you ready to leave now?"

"Yeah, let's go. Doris, I will see you later. Tell the children I said hello, especially the twins," said Lois.

When we got outside, Desi said, "Lois, I saw Dan about a month ago. He had on a marine's uniform, talking about he was just coming from boot camp. That boy ain't even old enough to be in no marines, is he?"

As we got in the car, Lois said, "Evidently, he is. His birth certificate says he is nineteen. He went in when he was eighteen. They had his birthdate wrong, so I got it straighten out for him before he went to New York. Anyway, let's talk about something else. Give me some money so I can get Terry some new sneakers and some clothes too."

Desi reached into his pocket and pulled out his money and asked, "How much so you need? Is twenty dollars enough?"

"No! I need about fifty dollars. I want to get me something too," said Momma.

So he peeled off another twenty and a ten-dollar bill and handed it to her.

Momma said, "You can just drop us off. We'll catch a cab home. I don't like Coleman to think anything something is going on with us. You know I married him. And besides, you are married and was married the whole time I was seeing you. I'm not going to be like that. Anyway, thanks for the ride, and for looking out for Terry. "Terry, say bye. You too, Chuckie."

Both said bye, and we got out of the car. Desi said, "Bye John Junior, see you later. I love you." As he pulled off, I asked, "Who is John Junior, Momma?"

"He was talking about you. His name is John Desi Atkinson. He just said that because he is your daddy, and if we were married when you're born, that's what your name would have been," said Momma.

I said, "Well, I am glad that's not my name. I like my name. I am a Bullock, just like Dan."

Momma bought Chuckie two pairs of shoes, a white pair of All-Stars and a black pair, also a new white pair for me. She even bought her a pair of loafers and a pair of sandals. Momma called a cab, and when it came, we all got into it and went home. Reverend Coleman was sitting on the front porch, reading his Bible. We spoke to him and went inside. Momma stayed outside, talking to Reverend Coleman. We could smell the cake as soon as we walked into the house and saw it on the kitchen table. Chuckie was delighted. Momma came into the kitchen and lit the seven candles, then told Chuckie to make a wish, and blow out the candles. Chuckie closed his eyes and seemed to be in deep concentration, then he inhaled and blew out all the candles at one time.

When Momma asked him what he had wished for, he said, "I wish for God to let Dan come back home in one piece."

Momma had tears in her eyes when she hugged him. Then she said, "After y'all eat a piece of cake, put on your new sneakers. Chuckie Coleman wants to tell you something after you get your sneakers on, okay?"

Chuckie said, "Yes, ma'am."

Just as we put our new sneakers on, Momma and Reverend Coleman walked into our room and told Chuckie to look on the back porch. We both went to the back porch, and there stood a brand-new shiny red bicycle, almost like mine, but smaller.

Momma started singing, "Happy birthday to you! Happy birthday to you! Happy birthday, dear Chuckie, happy birthday to you. Terry, I know you are happy too. Now you don't have to pull him on your bike everywhere you go. Help him get it off the porch, and here's a dollar for you and one for you, Chuckie. Y'all, ride to the store and buy some ice cream or something. Be careful." And off we rode side by side as we would do together for many years to come.

During the next week, when I got home from school, as soon as I walked into the house, I could hear Momma talking to Reverend Coleman. She sounded very happy as I walked into the living room. Reverend Coleman was smiling too.

Momma said, "Terry, guess what? I got a letter from Dan today. He said to tell you hello, and that he doesn't have any holes in him yet. He said some of his men got killed. He didn't know them. But I just pray that the Lord will continue to bless and protect him. I am so glad to hear from him and to know that he is all right. I am going to write him back, so you sit down and write him too. I will send it out tomorrow, so make sure you write him after you eat. Let me call Pete and tell her that I got this letter."

I said, "Can I read the letter?"

Momma handed the letter to Terry, then picked up the phone and called Aunt Pete. After reading the letter, Terry went into the kitchen, where Chuckie was eating. Momma came into the kitchen and started to fix the plates of meatloaf, mashed potatoes, and sweet peas. Momma said, "I called Pete, and she got a letter from Dan too. Bill told Pete that Dan was in Company F, and that F stood for fox. And he is in the Second Battalion, and some other long names. He said he would write to us once or twice a week. Pete said he sure didn't write very much other than somebody got killed, and he doesn't have any holes in him yet, and hello to Tony and Greg. Like he expect to have some holes in him or something. Her letter was just like mine, but I didn't see it that way. Anyway, go on and eat, Terry, so you can start on your letter and help Chuckie to write one too."

I said, "Yes, ma'am."

It was only a few days later, on a Saturday, another letter arrived. I knew it was from Dan because I saw that red, white, and blue stamp on it as the mail man put the letter in the mailbox. I got the letter and took it in the house and handed it to Momma. She was surprised and looked as if she was about to cry as she opened the letter.

I said, "Momma, what's wrong?"

She said, "Nothing, I'm just surprised Dan wrote again so soon. I am just happy to hear from him, and I get emotional just thinking about him. I will be so glad when he comes back home, and he's only been over there about a week and a half. He still got a long way to go, if he is going to be over there for a year. Lord knows I pray all the time. I can't help but worry about him." She turned the radio off, sat down, opened the letter, and started to read it. We watched her as she read the letter, which only took a few seconds. It was a one-page letter, just like the other one.

I asked, "Momma, did he say anything about my letter that I wrote to him?"

Lois said, "No, he didn't. He probably hadn't gotten your letter yet. He'll say something in his next letter, even though it goes by air-mail. It still takes a while for the mail to get there. This letter is just like the last letter, saying the same thing. But I am glad to hear from him as always. At least he is alive and well. Thank God."

Tony and Greg came into the house, and Tony said, "Hey, Aunt Lois, Momma told me to tell you that she got another letter from Dan today. It was just like the other one that she got las week."

Lois said, "Hey, Tony, come and hug my neck. You too, Greg." After she hugged them, she said, "I got a letter today too, just like the other one. Just like I was telling Terry, I am glad to hear from him, and I know that Pete is too. What is Reggie doing? I know he is just smiling with his pretty self? Chuckie, you and Greg, stop making all that noise before you wake Rocky up. Go on outside and play. Go ride your bikes."

I said, "Come on, Tony, let's ride to School Street School and see who is over there playing basketball."

Tony said, "Reggie is asleep. He is okay though. Come on, Terry. I would race you over there, but Greg and Chuckie can't keep up with us yet."

Momma said, "Y'all better be careful, and don't stay over there too long."

I said, "Yes, ma'am," and Tony repeated, and they both rushed out the door.

Momma and Aunt Porter would try calling New York so they could talk to Gloria but could never get an answer. They both loved family and was determined to keep the family together. Dan was the same way; he wanted to have everyone under the same roof. Somehow, he felt that it brings Momma back. But he desperately wanted Gloria back with Lois and Pete., and not all the way in Brooklyn, New York. And now Lois and Pete felt the distance with Dan being over in Vietnam. Their conversations were always pertaining to their fear for Dan and how surreal it all seemed. And oftentimes, the question of how Dan's birth certificate was altered came up, a subject Lois would always avoid. And they never failed to pray together and ask God (in the name of Jesus Christ) to continue to bless and protect Dan, and even Gloria in New York.

As I approached the house, I could see Uncle Bill and Aunt Porter's car in front of the house. I quickly walked up the stairs, opened the door, and went inside. Before I got to the living room, I could hear Momma and Aunt Porter talking.

Momma was saying, "I do love Coleman. He is a man of God, and he is nice to me and my children. Girl, I ain't thinking about Desi and no other man. But I know that Terry needs to know and see his daddy. So I have to see him at times, and Coleman knows that, Pete."

Aunt Pete said, "Girl, I just want to make sure that you keep a happy home. Because we have got to keep a home for our children. Daddy and Momma ain't here for us no more. But I am proud of you, and you are right, Reverend Coleman is a good man. You just hold on to him. He's good for you. Be nice to him. After all, he is your husband." Then she started to laugh, and Momma joined in with her. Then Aunt Porter said, "I almost forgot, I came over here to see if you got a call from Brooklyn, New York. When I was at work yesterday, Greg said the phone ranged, and when he picked it up, a White woman was on the other end, saying something about a long-distance call, so he hung up the phone. I wonder if it was Dan, or Gloria. Probably Gloria. So if you get a long-distance call, and if it is Dan or Gloria, tell them to call me back."

Lois said, "I sure will. It was probably Gloria, I pray that she is all right too. Lord knows I'll be just praying up something, especially for Dan. And you let me know too if you hear from them again. Pete, you know that I love you, don't you?"

Aunt Porter said, "Girl, I know you love me, just like you know that I love you too. Well, I better get home before Reggie wakes up and cook before Bill gets home. I will call you later. Terry, what are doing? Eavesdropping?"

Lois said, "I told him about doing that. Terry, you better stop being nosy and trying to listen to everybody's conversation. I know that you want to know what's going on with Dan. Just ask. Don't be eavesdropping. Now go to your room and change your school clothes, take them new sneakers off. Pete, call me. I got to get in here and cook too for my children before Coleman gets home. I'm glad Rocky is still asleep. Well, I'll see you later. Tell the children I love then, and hello to Bill."

"Okay, I will," said Aunt Porter. Then she went to her car and drove off.

Momma and Aunt Porter talked every day on the phone; sometimes it seemed like for hours. However, on this day, in mid-June, I heard the phone rang, and then Momma screamed unlike anyone I had ever heard screamed before. I raced into the living room, and she was on the floor. Momma kept screaming over and over, "No, no, no, it can't be! Lord, please let them be wrong. Oh no, no, not Dan!"

Chuckie and I tried to help her off the floor and also to console her. But she went on like that until she got tired, then she sat in the chair, moaning. We cried with her, not fully understanding magnitude of her pain.

Reverend Coleman was sitting on the porch, reading his Bible. He rushed into the living room and said, "Lois what is wrong? Are you all right?"

Still crying, she said, "Coleman, Pete called me and told me that Dan was killed on June 7, 1969. She said Daddy called her crying and told her just a few minutes ago, then she called me. I just don't believe it. We always pray that the Lord will protect Dan. How could something like that be true?"

Chuckie and I started to really cry, now that we understood that Dan was killed in the Vietnam War.

It was about two weeks later when Sergeant Galloway came to Uncle Bill and Aunt Porter's house. He was dressed in his marine dress blues, tall and handsome. Sergeant Galloway was the marine that escorted Dan's body back from Vietnam. He told Aunt Porter and Lois that Dan's body was at Hamilton Funeral Home. And that Dan would have a twenty-one-gun salute. Dan will have full honors. He said it was not just his duty, but an honor. Also, if anyone have any questions, he will try his best to answer them.

Momma said, "Well, we are grateful to you, and you are invited to dinner. Let me introduce you to some of the family. I am Lois, Dan's oldest sister. My husband sitting over there, reading his Bible, Reverend Artis Coleman. Then there is Porter, sitting on her husband's lap, which is Mr. William Bell. He is soldier and a paratrooper at that. We all call him Bill. Gloria is the youngest. She's in Brooklyn, New York. Daddy, Mr. Brother Bullock, is also in New York. They will be down here tomorrow.

Sergeant Galloway said, "I look forward meeting them both. And I sincerely thank you all for the hospitality."

It seems that the family cried and cried so much in the past two week that now they seem to be celebrating Dan's homecoming in heaven. That's what Reverend Coleman has been telling everyone who will listened. I heard Momma say that God wanted Dan to be in heaven with him, and not in a war overseas in Vietnam.

When we went to Hamilton Funeral Home to view Dan's body. As I approached the coffin, I saw that there was a glass top over Dan's body, and I could see him very clearly. He didn't look like Dan at all. The person in that casket was fat and really big. But we would all learn from Sergeant Galloway that Dan's body was bloated because the body releases gases and because he had to travel for days in the glass enclosure. His explanation seemed to satisfy everyone.

On the day of Dan's burial, the family all lined up to get into the limousines. Once we arrived at the cemetery, we sat in chairs, facing Dan's casket. Many people were standing. Then three of the marines performed a twenty-one-gun salute. I made up mind to ask Sergeant Galloway why only three marines instead of twenty-one marines doing the twenty-one-gun salute.

After the funeral, we all went back over to Aunt Porter's house. I looked for Sergeant Galloway, but I never saw again. I guess he did his duty and left. Well, I knew that Uncle Bill knows, so when I saw him sitting by himself, I walked over to him.

"Uncle Bill, why does a twenty-one-gun salute only have three marines performing the ceremony?" I asked.

Uncle Bill said, "Terry, I don't even believe that the higher-ups in Washington even know. I have heard so many reasons that I quit trying to keep up with them."

I said, "That's what I thought, Uncle Bill. I knew that you would answer my question. Thank you. I was going to ask Sergeant Galloway, but I didn't see him after the funeral. He probably didn't even know anyway. Well, at least Dan is in heaven now."

Uncle Bill said, "That's right, Terry. Dan is in heaven with the Lord now, smiling down on all of us, and don't forget that he took his secret to the grave with him. This is just the beginning of Dan's legacy."

The newspapers from New York to Goldsboro and all across the nation was talking about Dan going into the marines at the tender age of fourteen years old and being the youngest killed in Vietnam at the age of fifteen years old. And the legacy begins…

ABOUT THE AUTHOR

Nathan Terry Bullock was born in Goldsboro, North Carolina, on July 23, 1958, to Dan's oldest sister Lois Bullock (when she was only fifteen years old), and his father is John Desi Atkinson. Terry, as he was so fondly called, grew up in the same household with his grandparents, mother, uncle—Dan—and aunts, Porter and Gloria.

Nathan started writing about Dan because all his life, he has been somewhat lost and empty on the inside since Dan was killed in action in Vietnam when he was forty-five days from his tenth birthday. Nathan also wanted his children and grandchildren, also family and America, to know the ultimate sacrifice that PFC Dan Bullock made for his country.

Moreover, Dan was not only Nathan's uncle, but his brother and best friend. Nathan would follow Dan everywhere he went, which he shares about Dan's life and the escapades he experienced, along with the tragedies of hurt and loss in his young life. Yet his love for family and zest for life only seemed to have increased after a tragedy or loss.

After sharing excerpts with family and a few friends, Nathan was encouraged to have his manuscript submitted for publishing. Having been accepted, Nathan has become a first-time published author.